Super Vita-Minds

How to STOP Saying, I *Hate* You… To Yourself!

"A Spiritual Facelift!"

Super Vita-Minds

**How To STOP Saying, I *Hate* You…
To Yourself!**

DAYA DEVI-DOOLIN

CasAnanda Publishing
New York Florida

Super Vita-Minds: How To STOP Saying, I *Hate* You... To Yourself!

P. O. Box 4267, Enterprise, FL 32725-0267.

Library of Congress Catalog Card Number: 98-93137
ISBN 1-889131-23-7

First Edition 1997
1 2 3 4 5 6 7 8 9 10

Other Books by Rev. Daya Devi-Doolin:
Dabney's Handbook on A Course in Miracles
All I Need to Know...Is Inside (A Pocket Bite Book)
Returning to the Source (book of poems)Dormck
Dabney, Dormck & Wiggles Slakaduman Adventures
Dormck and the Temple of the Healing Light
Sikado's Star of Aragon (Dabney & Dormck Adventures)

Printed in the United States of America

Cover Design by Daya Devi-Doolin
Edited by Lydia Bandini

CasAnanda Publishing
POB 7207
Bayonet Point, Fl 34674

Printed in the U.S.A.
Morris Publishing • 3212 E. Highway 30 • Kearney, NE 68847

Super Vita-Minds

How To STOP Saying I *Hate* You...
To Yourself!

DAYA DEVI-DOOLIN

Padaran Publications
Enterprise, FL 32725

PUBLISHER'S NOTE

The publisher and author shall have neither liability nor responsibility to any person or organization with respect to any loss or damage caused or alleged to be caused directly or indirectly by the information contained in this book. The purpose of this book is to educate, entertain and stimulate.

This book is sold with the understanding that the publisher and author are not involved in offering legal, medical or psychological services. If any assistance is required, the services of a competent professional should be sought. In addition, it is not the purpose of this book to be used in the diagnosis of any medical or psychological condition.

DEDICATION

To my three bright stars who landed on earth, my husband Chris and my two sons, Tyler and Joseph. To my parents, Sallie and Leon Brown who have shown only love, peace, strength and support. To my mother in-law, Mary Carty Doolin who has been like a second mother to me and is very supportive of my creativeness. To Christ who has been branded in my heart since childhood, Mother Mary, Kwan Yin, my Reiki Guides and my other Ascended Master friends of the Fifth Dimension.

TABLE OF CONTENTS

ACKNOWLEDGMENTS..........XII

PREFACE..........XIII

FOREWORD..........XVI

INTRODUCTION..........XVII

CHAPTER 1
Your *I Am* Consciousness..........1

Super Beings Speak. The Gift of the I AM Presence. You can have everything. Faith in illusions. Drawing a check on the Bank of Heaven. Which I AM consciousness am I choosing? How to be free from strife. I AM. How to be free of ego and its games.

CHAPTER 2
Right-Minded Seeing..........11

Right-Mindedness/Wrong-Mindedness. How do we invite right mindedness? Lack equals itself. Am I better than you? How to change someone. How to seal your spoken word. How to stop mis-creating.

CHAPTER 11
Immaculate Conception....................................139

Personal journaling concerning intention and its application. Conversations with Ascended Master Kwan Yin. Conversations with Ascended Master Ezekiel. Conversations with Ascended Master Mother Mary.

CHAPTER 12
Weep Not, Nor Faint....................................151

Excerpts from my personal journal on the power of intention and its application. Finding our way home. Joseph, Father of Jesus. The next hurdle. The "Right" parents. Summary.

APPENDIX....................................160

Summary. Worksheets and Exercises. Journaling Pages. Poems. Meditations. Information for Transformational Spiritual Growth. Glossary of Alternative Healing Modalities. Glossary. Recommended Books. Index.

ILLUSTRATIONS
Fig. 1.1....................................5

ACKNOWLEDGMENTS

I wish to acknowledge and thank my soul mate, best friend, the stepfather and father of my two sons, my husband Chris, for his unselfish support in the writing of my books, music and in the healing profession to which I have been called. He has been extremely balanced, caring, loving, responsible and understanding on all levels. I deeply appreciate his love and wisdom for our children and myself.

I thank all of you who have come into my life and enriched it with your words, hugs and kisses, support, experiences, tears, laughter and wisdom. I would like to thank my editor and dear sweet spiritual "sister", Lydia Bandini for her superb workmanship of **Super Vita-Minds: How To Stop Saying I Hate You...To Yourself!**, to Dr. William W. Whitson of the Foundation for Inner Peace for permission to use quotes of **A Course in Miracles (ACIM)**. Thanks to the Brown, Doolin and Watson Family, especially my brother Lee who is responsible for showing me another dimension when I was nineteen. Thanks to Monetta Harris and Shirley Satterfield, my two dear longtime friends since college, Mae Vershier; Cathy McDonald a staunch supporter of The Doolin Healing Sanctuary and our family since the first day of Joseph; Diane Fisher and Frank Carolei. Thanks to Rev. Carolyn Schinzel, for her additional editorial comments, Dr. Christopher and Rev. Merci Jordan, Gail Fleming, Bob and Iris Reynolds, Patricia Collins, Rev. Carol Jo Garfinkel, my Reiki Master Teachers, Donna Snow Spears, Lisa Lloyd and Rev. Dr. Constance Johnson. My gratitude to Mary Stinson, my "spiritual sister", who opened the door to my Reiki path, Janna Bensko, my Reiki student graduates and a list too long to mention, but I know you all know who you are. I am very grateful for your love. I thank my long-time friend, Michael Robins for the beautiful Foreword, to my friend and teacher, I. Jared Rosen, for his personal endorsement and to Bobbi Janson of CasAnanda Publishing for being the "midwife" for the birth of my book. Specifically, I thank my husband Chris for supporting my long, long nights, for being Mr. "Mom" sometimes and for his keen editorial skills. Thank you for "squeezing" time <u>out</u> of time to make this book a success!

I love you!

PREFACE

I have been a student of **A Course in Miracles**, since 1986. I later became a co-facilitator of the Course with Chris. Every day I have rejoiced over the new me that has emerged each and every day since then. My spiritual growth has been non-stop and is as exciting as witnessing a baby being delivered.

My life's been completely charged with many, many blessings. If ever I find myself reverting back to old habits of thinking, I can no longer stay with them for more than a minute. I have been given too many tools that enable me to look beyond all illusions that try to surface.

I now look straight into the thought pattern that might be trying to control and limit me and I send it packing. I've had help in being able to do this. The Holy Spirit guides my new thought system that enables me to do all that I do.

My ego was not about to let up its control so easily. If it found that my new consciousness was totally in control of a particular situation, it would say, "Well, I know where I can stick her. I know her weak points or I'll create some situation so I can be in control of her mind again. I can start bellyaching about being in an accident, being harmed and being involved in something harmful. I'll get her to worry here because she watches too many cop programs, murder mysteries and the like. She must be fearful here, so that's where I'll attack her mind and take away her peace."

Today, I can look at the small ego and say "That is nonsense. I am totally, completely and fully protected by the Source of all Life. Christ's Light enfolds me". I can call forth the Light and ***know*** only Good exists. I can call forth the truth of "I Am One with God." The small sunbeam (ego) is then transmuted and transformed by Truth into nothingness.

I have aligned myself with the Power of God and so I know where my strength lies. I know the Power that thoughts have. Many, many people are not yet aware of the power of their thoughts. If my thoughts are not productive and constructive, I get rid of them by releasing them. I basically say good-bye. I do not give them anymore attention or energy. I do not embrace their imprint or allow them to manifest their results in my life.

Many times I have heard myself thinking, "I wish people knew that they do have the power to change their world and their lives just by changing their thoughts and attitude. I wish I could tell them that there is hope and that there is a solution to their problems. If only they knew the benefits of knowing how to control their thoughts. If only they knew that positive thoughts produce the good they want; negative thoughts bring the circumstances that cause them misery."

I am now realizing that I can help others to realize this as I have been helped to come into this realization as well. I can help others by affirming the truth about others and myself. The Truth is that we are One with Christ. We are all Christ-like, because we contain the Christ Consciousness within the DNA matrix of our being. I know that existing problems are resolved once everyone realizes he is not separate from Universal Mind, Yahweh, Creator or God.

We grow up believing we can be hurt. We accept that world consciousness, unconsciously. We pass it on to our children and they believe it. They buy into it. Some of us grow up believing we are stupid, ugly, no good, dumb, evil, clumsy, lazy, forgetful, too fat, too skinny, too talkative, not talkative enough or shy and these beliefs pass on from generation to generation. But we can stop this...Now!

We can say, "No. That's not me any more. No. I do not believe what you say about me. I know I am good. I know that I am beautiful and loving. I know I am special and I am important, regardless of anyone's perception about me. I am invulnerable. I am harmless nor can I be harmed by anyone."

We can say, "STOP! I WILL NOT ALLOW YOU TO SPEAK TO ME OR ABUSE ME ANY LONGER!"

This book was written to give people *permission* to remember that they can stop believing they need to hate themselves any longer. You can now choose to stop believing and saying you are less that anyone else. You can now stop buying into lack, limitation, poverty, sickness, disease and loneliness. You can start remembering that you are Light. You are Abundance. You are Love. You are Enough!

My book, **Super Vita-Minds: How to Stop Saying, I Hate You...To Yourself!** contains powerful affirmations of Truth that can revitalize your whole spiritual, mental, emotional and physical structures. They can raise the vibratory signature of the subatomic particles of your entire being. You can now begin to radiate at a higher frequency of Universal Light waves which attract more Light energy experiences into your awareness and body.

Through taking one - two caplets of **Super Vita-Minds** (a power packed positive thought form) every day, you will begin to find your whole life becoming more meaningful, loving, safe and harmless.

Take one or two caplets of **Super Vita-Minds** tonight and call me in the morning! Be good to the beautiful self you already are. Now you can begin saying, **I Love Me!**

I Love You!

Daya.

FOREWORD

It is a great honor and privilege to be asked to write this foreword. But I intuit that I will continue to appreciate the fruits of this opportunity as time passes, because Daya is profoundly in touch with the deep mystery of life in a natural way that significantly affects all those who come into her Energy field.

I have known Daya for a long time, but in reading **Super Vita-Minds**, I learned more about Daya's personal life than I had in the years of association with her. It's remarkable how little I knew about her personal life. However, I have always known her to be Rock-Solid in the Christ experience. I have never seen her one iota out of alignment with the Perfection Gift. And her service of love's healing is always available, insightful and helpful. She has been a blessing to many and has made significant and lasting contributions in my life. Once, I stayed in her home for a few days. It was a Holy experience. I can't really describe in words but my finances soared and I was rather disappointed when I had to leave.

So I hope I have conveyed that there is something remarkable and special about Daya and I believe anyone who comes in contact with this book is fortunate. If they read it, they're even more fortunate. And if they undertake a serious study and application of the ideas presented in it their blessings will be great.

Daya shows up for me as a powerful Christ; yet she's giggly and totally natural and unassuming. She is a role model of our rich, Infinite possibility manifesting. She is a forerunner and pioneer of the new order of life that is imminent and emerging on the planet while the news media is still full of stories of calamity, chaos and fear. The Real News continues to transform lives into ones of peace and happiness. We have reached a critical mass of understanding and realizing the Christ message and the fruits are everywhere. **Super-Vita-Minds** is one of those fruits and it may be a means of reminding you of that often overlooked statement that is naturally talking to you, "What I have done, you shall do and even greater things." Happy reading!

Michael Robins, Awakener of your heart's purpose and. Oneness Appreciator (407) 539-655.

INTRODUCTION

With the information in this book, you can finally start saying I love you to yourself and start living an enjoyable life. You will receive a wealth of information and go on an exciting trip into yourself, perhaps for the first time.

You will be taught the skills of affirming "I Love You" to yourself! You will be shown how to overcome abusive behavior towards yourself and towards others.

The law of cause and effect will be explained in a contemporary, easy and practical way for you to utilize in your life, making every situation a winning one.

If you read this book carefully and apply the techniques offered, you can begin to consistently experience being the Master of your life and loving what you are creating. You will be winning at life because you will love yourself and others more and more unconditionally. You will be shown how to win at loving yourself and how to consistently see things manifest that *you desire* because the law of cause and effect will have become your law as well.

No longer will you want to consciously or unconsciously sabotage yourself with your words, thoughts or deeds. You will be a winner and all your experiences will prove that to you. I will be glad to hear about your new self, so please feel free to write to me.

Are you ready to get started?

Super Vita-Minds

How to STOP Saying, I *Hate* You… To Yourself!

Daya Devi-Doolin

The Reservoir of Life

I AM the reservoir of life
Its dance is
To fill me up.
I cannot allow a
Doubt or fear or hate
To fill my cup,
Or life will not flow,
It can't remain
And I will
Lose my place.

I AM the reservoir of life
Its dance is
To fill me up.
I let it flow
And fill my space,
It makes me sing
I gain my place.

Life can't flow
If I'm full of holes
Of doubts and fears and worry.
But I will sing
When I believe
There is no need for sorrow.

I AM the reservoir of life.

Daya Devi-Doolin

CHAPTER ONE

YOUR I AM CONSCIOUSNESS

Super Beings Speak

Two years before this book actually was started in 1989, I was told in the *silence*, I would be writing a book called **Super Vita-Minds: How to Stop Saying I Hate You...To Yourself**! A lot of transformation has taken place in my life since then as I'm sure it has in yours. You are at a place now where you are clearly ready for more Truth and more mysteries to be unraveled to your soul. I am glad to be here to help offer assistance on your journey.

It has been revealed to me during my transformation that we have Super Beings, Ascended Masters as they are called by some, and Angelic Hosts by others that have been guiding me long before I knew they existed in the invisible realm. They have been guiding me in the writing of all my previous books. For this honor, I am very grateful.

They know which words, which truths are needed by you at this time to raise your consciousness to the next level. I now share what they would have us know together as speakers for God.

When I started writing this book, It was my intention to be able to write in the clearest and simplest form possible about the I Am Consciousness that would enable you, the reader, to grasp its fullest meaning. I therefore called upon our Ascended Masters of the White Brotherhood, the Holy Angelic Beings, for assistance.

I spoke the following invocation for grace and assistance and thereby the understanding of the rest of this book. I said, "I charge my Presence with the qualities of the Ascended Masters, Jesus Christ, Blessed Mother Mary, Kuthumi, Zoser, St. Germain and all the rest of the Great Brotherhood to guide my writing of this chapter and the rest of this book. I sense your Presence, the help I need and so I know It Is under Grace. I am thankful for your blessings."

The Gift Of The I AM Presence

The channeling I received in response was, "We call upon you to explain to the masses that they are not alone. They have been given the gift of the I AM Presence; the HOLY Gift. This means that no one can say, "I AM" without getting the results she wants. Mankind was given this gift to bring about only that which is good in this life, but he has misused his power on a lower level". (He has used this power to mis-create his world and bring upon his own misery.)

You Can Have Everything

They continued, "Dear Children, pick up your skirts of illusions and walk with us. You can have everything you want by using your I AM Power. Instead of calling forth destruction as in calling forth "I AM SICK", call forth the qualities of Light by saying for example, "I Am WHOLE - I AM LIGHT.

All I AM statements are your level of mind consciousness, your level of awareness, your trust in the universe. Your I AM PRESENCE puts you in tune with your Oneness to that which you speak or invoke. I AM SICK calls forth sickness. I AM BROKE calls forth lack of supply. I AM ALONE calls forth the qualities of loneliness. Your faith in your I AM statement is honored by the universe even though your statements are illusions and are not recognized by us."

Faith In Illusions

"Your faith in your illusions begets the results that cannot make you happy. Lift up your voice as you speak, lift up your consciousness as you speak and we will answer your call. We are here to help all our brothers and sisters to reach mastery. It brings us great joy to serve you.

Be not doubtful, anxious or hardheaded. Your I AM PRESENCE is the most important gift you've been endowed with. It stands in the realm of Peace. It is God individualized as you in the flesh.

Once you have called on your I AM PRESENCE to destroy your reality of truth, then no one can keep you out of the dilemma until or unless you release your hold on the negative aspect of consciousness and speak the Word for a transmutation - a positive solution.

Baptize your mind, your consciousness with Cosmic Rays- streams of Light beams from the Center of the Universe. Lose yourself in the Center of God - get still and quiet. Listen to the stillness and become calm. Become Power-Full not Power-less. All life is consciousness at one level or another.

If we believe in the negative, which does not exist, it will manifest for us because we "believe" in it. If we turn the Light on our illusions, they will be shed as a tear and dropped away. Be at Peace, It is your Birthright.

Thank you,

Jesus Christ, Kuthumi, Zoser, St. Germain, Mother Mary and many more Angelic Hosts."

Drawing A Check On The Bank Of Heaven

Many people intuitively know that if they have a problem, there is always a way out if only they could find it. In Emmett Fox's booklet, **Life is Consciousness**, he tells us "The way out lies in the spoken word. In the bible the "Word" means any definitely formulated thought not just the drifting thought that floats through your mind. The Word is creative and the strongest and most creative word is "I am." When you say "I am", you are calling upon the universe to do something for you and it will do it. When you say, "I Am", you are drawing a check on the universe. It will be honored and cashed sooner or later and the proceeds will go to you. If you say, "I am tired, sick, poor, fed up, disappointed, getting old," you are drawing checks for future trouble and limitation. When you say, "I am divine life", "I am divine truth", "I am divine freedom", "I am substance", "I am eternal substance", you are drawing a check on the bank of Heaven, and surely that check will be honored with health and plenty for you. Whatever you associate yourself with, you bring into your consciousness."

When we listen to the ego's voice that we created, we hear and act on all the confusing disharmony it provides for us. We are too busy to hear or acknowledge the Holy Spirit's Voice within us. All that we focus on we then magnify into our world as our 'truth.' Most often we dislike what we have chosen to embrace after we see the manifestation of it, but we have created it and we can also delete it and make something anew.

WHICH I AM CONSCIOUSNESS AM I CHOOSING?

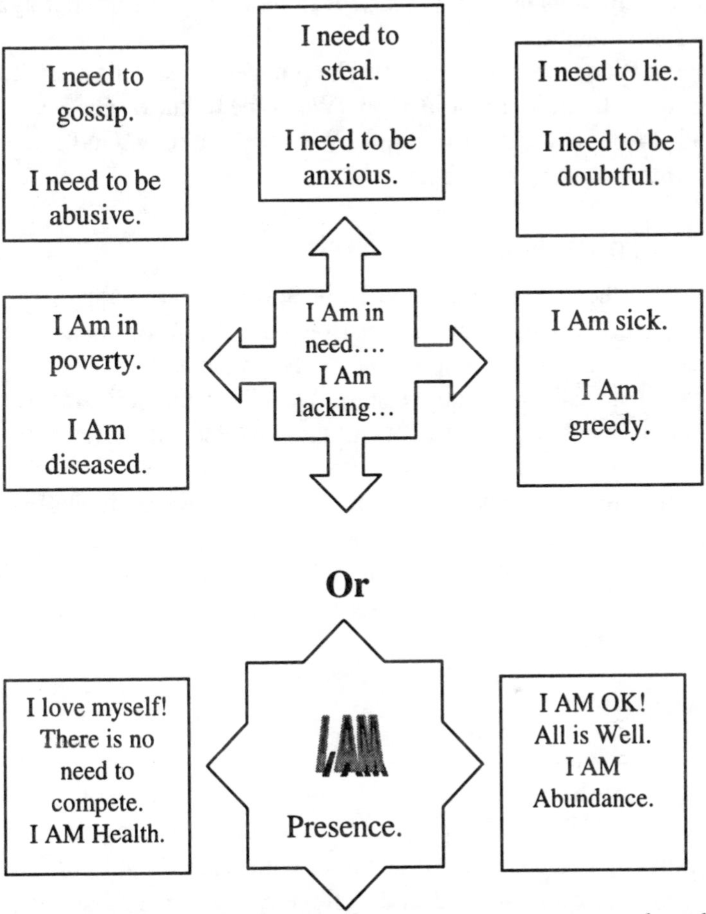

Fig. 1.1 *Nodules in top illustration represent erroneous thought patterns that attract negativity to itself and gives a false sense of security, but without substance or happiness. The nodules below point to thought patterns of strong vibrational energy, which make you the Master of your life and attract experiences that empower you.

Depression has many rooms. The many levels of it only exist in our own minds. We choose which rooms we want to pay for. The rent keeps going up and we continue to pay through our fears. They increase, bind us up and increase even more until we are paralyzed in one form or another.

When we cannot handle the plugged up situation any longer, then we call out, but that is good. We come to know who we are as a result of our separation in mind. We come to know God is there all the time and always has been.

How To Be Free From Strife

When we listen to the Holy Spirit, we are happy, free from strife, vibrate health, are fully sustained with no effort and become capable of doing the impossible. The miracles then become daily occurrences all the time because we allow the universe to work through us rather than reject what the universe has for us. By doing this we release our grip on the meaningless world we've mis-created. Anytime we are ready to have our prayers answered it shall be done right then and there, for God is without time. We have a backlog of answered prayers waiting for us to redeem when we are no longer frightened of having them answered, or feel we don't deserve to have them answered.

I AM

Whatever we put our I AM consciousness to, whatever we believe in, the LAW of God that works through our subconscious level, is fulfilled. The purpose of our subconscious was to fill our lives with only good, to fill our lives with what we put our faith into. But we have turned it around believing in the negative so strongly that the LAW has to fulfill ITSELF in our lives according to the faith we put into our belief. The LAW responds in no other way.

There are many, many games ego will play with you if you choose to get caught up in them. See if you recognize any of these games in your life. These games keep you from knowing peace, harmony, abundance, love and faith in the TRUTH while you have faith in fear (lack).

- I wonder what's going to go wrong today?
- Is my child safe? What's out there...to hurt him?
- How will I survive if I give this up?
- How will I earn a living if I do what I want and love to do?
- Why am I always so poor?
- Why do I have so many bills?
- Why do I have to work so hard for so little?
- Why does he have more than I have?
- Why does my car always break down?
- Why do auto mechanics always cheat you?

How To Be Free Of Ego And Its Games

"Jesus' resurrection means that He transcended ego. He did not attack it. By attacking, we make whatever lack we believe in real in our minds, so we can never overcome it by our own will. But we can transcend ego and take back the power we gave to it. It will remain as the nothing it was before we gave our power to it to govern us.

We do this by surrendering our "stubborn" will to the Will of the Holy Spirit, to be erased from our minds forever. We do this by releasing our hold onto the illusions of our "problem". We take a dose or two of **Super Vita-Mind** caplets.

We have to desire to forgive ourselves for creating the problem. We have to desire to forgive ourselves for holding onto the problem and we have to choose to do so. Then we need to ask the Holy Spirit to erase all of our error thoughts about the problem we thought we had. When we do this we can then see the solution which has always been there waiting for us to accept.

We have to be willing to put our faith in the TRUTH instead of illusion. We make illusion real by our faith in it, but it is not anything. We do not have to do anything when we put our faith in

TRUTH. TRUTH just is. When we make our illusions real, we have to project our justifications onto them to prove to ourselves that what we feel and see must be the TRUTH because we believe in it.

Our steps to transcending ego:

- I AM no longer afraid of ego, my little self.
- I AM absolutely certain that I trust in the TRUTH.
- I AM absolutely certain there can be no lack in my life.
- I AM absolutely certain I AM without fear of any kind.
- I AM absolutely certain I want to surrender all my thoughts to the Holy Spirit for purification in return for the gifts of joy, peace of mind, love and forgiveness.
- I forgive everyone and every situation from the past, present and future. I release them to receive their good and I loose myself from unforgiving thoughts towards myself.
- I thank the universe for the lessons I have learned from these experiences and I AM now ready to move on to receive my good.
- I surrender my will totally into the hands of the Holy Spirit." (*See References,* **Dabney's Handbook on A Course in Miracles,** Daya Devi-Doolin).

Your I AM Consciousness is VERY precious. Appreciate it and let it work for you for the good it was intended!

Brief Points of Chapter

- We have the Gift of the I AM Presence.
- We can have everything.
- Which I AM consciousness are you choosing for your way out?
- Draw your check on the Bank of Heaven.

- Release your grip on illusions and you faith will magnify.
- Begin to be free from strife by listening to the Holy Spirit.
- Steps you can take in transcending ego.

"I have crossed from the wilderness of this world, into the PROMISED LAND of plenty." *--Chris Doolin*

CHAPTER TWO

RIGHT-MINDED SEEING

"If nothing but the Truth exists, right minded seeing cannot see anything but perfection." **(ACIM)**

Right-Mindedness/Wrong-Mindedness

According to the Teacher's Manual of **ACIM,** "Right-mindedness listens to the Holy Spirit, forgives the world and through Christ's vision sees the real world in its place. This is the final vision, the last perception and the condition in which God takes the final step Himself. Here time and illusions end together. Wrong-mindedness listens to the ego and makes illusions real; perceiving sin and justifying anger, and seeing guilt, disease and death as real. Both this world and the real world are illusions because right mindedness merely overlooks, or forgives what never happened."

How Do We Invite Right-Mindedness?

We could choose to invite the Holy Spirit to correct all our error thoughts or wrong-mindedness by:

Before arising in the morning and upon retiring at night you could choose to say:

- I surrender all my past thoughts, my present thoughts and my future thoughts into the hands of the Holy Spirit and I AM thankful.
- I surrender my will into the Hands of the Holy Spirit this day.
- I surrender my stubborn will into the hands of the Holy Spirit.
- I release all my problems, fears or mis-creations into the Hands of the Holy Spirit.
- I am willing to release my worries, my will over to my Comforter.

You will begin to feel the completion of your prayer being fulfilled when you do it and do so with feeling. When you feel the Presence as you get quiet you will KNOW THAT YOU KNOW YOU KNOW; IT IS DONE. You will no longer have poor relationships with anyone. You'll be looking into the center of the Light at all things. You will be seeing with right mindedness.

I frequently hear such comments as, "...this person at work won't behave the way he's supposed to," or "My wife thinks I never do anything right," or "That person is always mean, loud or rude." They may also talk about how their daughter or son is full of trouble, or that they are selfish. They complain of their job or a certain ailment that plagues them. The list goes on and on.

Lack Equals Itself

I have found what some people don't realize is that what they are really saying is that they believe in lack. Lack is the idol they have faith in. They have proclaimed lack and they believe in it. They have faith in *it*. They don't realize that since they believe in lack, lack has to manifest itself to them as an out-picturing of their thoughts. They are choosing to believe what their eye sees, what their egos (surface mind) sees, rather than what is truth on the invisible plane.

The truth is that everything is already and always has been perfect. God has not made anything imperfect. We make what we see imperfect by our perception of it with our eyes and words.

The universe, according to our belief in a thing, will provide the effect of the cause rooted in our thinking. This proves to us that what we perceive to be true is true. That is how the Law of Substance (God-Mind) works.

Am I Better Than You?

Our ego loves to say that we are better than a particular person because we don't act like they do or dress like they do. The truth of the matter is, we are no better than anyone if we find ourselves standing in judgment upon her with no patience or forgiveness to offer. We see in others what we see in ourselves. The Course tells us, "No one can be unjust to you unless you have decided first to be unjust."

When we begin to see beyond the eyes of ego, with the eyes of our Christ-Mind, we will see that everyone is no different. We will see that we are all only loving beings, or beings that desire to be loved. When you see yourself as whole, you make no demands on others to be so, because you know they are whole as well.

How To Change Someone

If you feel you wish you could change someone or that he needs your help, the best way to help is to help yourself first by knowing the truth about that person in the Mind of God. Realize that this person is sinless in the Mind of God just as sure as you are as well. God judges no one.

If you wish to change someone, you will have to change your perception of him and your attitude about him. Then you help him to see himself differently. You will see him in the Light and his transformation can then take place. By letting go of trying to "help" him, you acknowledge that the Holy Spirit within him is guiding, helping, cleansing and healing him as well as It is helping you, healing and cleansing you.

How can you do this? You can do it by knowing and putting yourself in a consciousness of WE ARE ONE WITH GOD. By knowing this, then you proceed to know, to speak and affirm these statements for your friends, fellow workers, sister, other family members.

If you feel, for example, that you are in an unjust situation where your husband does not cooperate with you in spiritual growth and other matters, then write the following statement or a similar one in your words that you can relate to:

> My husband (write his name in blank)__________ ________, loves cooperating with me and I with him. We work together in love for each other's spiritual growth. I am grateful we are being shown how to do this.

Instead of believing the error thought, "My husband never cooperates with me," you take your consciousness out of surface mind (ego) and up into God-Mind immediately. By believing in the error thought, you perpetuate the very negative condition you think you see and wish did not exist.

By affirming the truth about the situation, you will draw the essence of cooperation that you desire. The universe only desires to give us all we desire according to our belief and faith. It WILL give you all you desire according to the feeling nature behind your faith.

What happens when you speak the Word, when you affirm the truth about a situation? What happens when you now say, "My husband (sister, wife) now cooperates fully with me and I with them." You will find:

- You won't be frustrated trying to force someone to do something you want done.
- You are not struggling or wrestling with not being "in control" of people or conditions.

- The situation will dissolve totally into truth because you are letting the Holy Spirit re-interpret your error thoughts into Truth.
- You will find the solution is in the problem. You just release your hold on how you look at the problem and turn it around to your good, your peace of Mind and theirs.

Most of all, you will find that right-minded seeing cannot see anything but perfection in anyone or anything. It is always our choice how we choose to react to what is happening. We can choose to be angry, mad and jealous while another in the same situation will choose to be happy regardless to what appears to be happening. You are now starting to say I love You…to yourself.

When you take your consciousness out of the realm of hate, anger and unhappiness with world conditions, and put your consciousness in the realm of I AM ONE WITH GOD, you will know only peace, happiness and compassion. When you stop getting joy out of being unhappy, you will know what real joy is in being unconditionally happy.

How To Seal Your Spoken Word

Now, you can seal your spoken word with this acknowledgment, "My husband, (co-worker, sister) now forgives me totally and I fully and freely forgive him and release him in love. I honor him for the teacher he has been to me." Forgiveness frees you to be unburdened by mistrust and hatred. It frees you to enjoy the love you know you ought to have. From the workbook of **ACIM**, "All forgiveness is a gift to yourself."

Your patience with someone else is the same as your patience with yourself. You are both children of God, and you are both worth the patience that a holy one deserves.

How To Stop Mis-creating

Do you feel that your finances are not in the state you would like them to be? If so, just realize that you have perceived a "lack" in your finances and so they would have to manifest itself as such because you believe it, giving it power by your Word and So It Is! This is what is called mis-creating rather than creating or being co-creators with God (Infinite Mind).

By claiming and decreeing, "My finances are always increasing and multiplying and so are my services to people in a harmonious way." you will change your direction. You must put faith and belief in a positive way behind your word in order to change your mind about your apparent situation of lack. You are not changing God's Mind, but you are telling Him you are ready to accept what He has already prepared for you as heir to His Kingdom. You are changing your mind, to "right minded" seeing.

If you choose to believe in what you think you see, evidence of lack of finances, or lack of material things or spiritual things, you are telling the universe that's what you wish to be provided with, the cause and effect of your thoughts.

Thoughts are substance and form. They draw unto themselves the likeness of their form. That is how we are made in the image of God. We have the power by our word to form all that we wish to create, or mis-create. If you do not like what your thoughts are presenting to you, then you have to change your thoughts, your consciousness. You have to live in the I AM ONE with joy, kindness, abundance, success consciousness if that is what appears lacking in your life.

Circle below which statement you would like to be a part of your life and you will see the universe will make it so.

- I live with abundance.
- I breathe in abundance.
- I love with abundance.
- I live with success.
- I breathe in success.
- I live with lack.
- I breathe lack.
- I lack love.
- I love lack.

- I lack success.
- I breathe in negativity.
- I breathe in love for myself.

Whatever thoughts we choose to live with in our consciousness is what has to manifest for us in the outer. That is how the law of cause and effect works. As you step into the next chapter, be willing to believe "I can surrender and see my beauty."

Brief Points of Chapter

- Invite right-minded seeing.
- See beyond the eyes of ego.
- Change someone by first changing your perception of her.
- Seal your spoken word.
- Start creating with God.
- Use the law of cause and effect with awareness and purpose.

Gift Of The Spirit

Joy is the gift of Spirit
To impose its ecstasy upon the soul.
Joy is mystical love wandering
From cell to cell of the universe.
So lift up the skirts of your heart,
Allow it to rush in.
Let it take control over you.
Be silly.
Laugh!
Surrender!

Daya Devi-Doolin,
Returning To The Source

CHAPTER THREE

SURRENDERING

How To Dissolve Negative Conditions

If you are in a situation, condition, or health problem you now believe you are in, this is an error thought you have decided to believe about yourself. When you deny what you think is real, you are denying the power of the error thought over you any longer. You are dissolving it from its existence in your life, and mind.

You are allowing the Holy Spirit to replace it with Truth into your consciousness. But until you deny that the illusion exists, you cannot find your way to the solution that is already present, NOW, and always has been there for you to accept.

Example I no longer live in the consciousness that energy is lacking in my body, mind, heart and affairs.

Example I now live in the consciousness that divine energy is freely flowing through my body, mind, heart and affairs.

What Is An Affirmation?

When you make an affirmation statement, you are making a positive statement to align yourself with the consciousness of a state of being that already exists for you. You are just re-membering this by repeating this and feeding it into your subconscious, your awareness. This is what is real, and not what you think unreal. You are ***claiming*** the truth about yourself.

This is not believing a lie as you may believe you are doing. You are not trying to coerce God to change your situation, but you are unifying your consciousness with HIS.

You know by your accepting your ONENESS with HIS LAW of MIND, you are accepting HIS truth about you, as you are one with HIM and all creation. "It is only your thoughts that cause you pain," (**ACIM**) and so you can re-think your thoughts into ones of positive-ness, JOY, and RELEASE from fear and pain.

When the Apostle, Paul wrote..."Awake, thou that sleepest and arise from the dead..." he meant for us to rid ourselves of error thought, negative thoughts, and then the truth can be established. It can shine down upon us and loose our sleep, our chains that have bound us from knowing true happiness. We will be free to see the beauty within us.

You can release yourself by this affirmation:

My error thoughts about ______________________________ ______________________(situation, person or condition) are now being corrected by the Holy Spirit within me and I am truly grateful. Everyday in every way my mortal limitations are being dropped away from my consciousness.

Would you rather say?

I am always sick.	or I am always well.
Everybody makes me sick.	or I live in complete harmony.
Nothing works for me.	or I fully accept all my good.

The weather is lousy.	or I am happy, rain shine.
I am always broke.	or God is my constant supply.
People always cheat me	or Everyone prospers me.

Which one of these statements makes you happy to say it? You can experience and live constantly in the present, knowing the positive statements above can change your life by the feeling and belief you put into knowing them.

These are not just words or a formula to act like magic. These are thought forms that attract the feeling nature of the same form from Divine Substance to manifest for you, because it is your inheritance to receive them.

Can The Body Think?

If you have believed a food or a particular kind of food such as bread or ice cream has a bad effect on you, guess again. If you believe food is what makes you overweight, guess again. If you believe everything you eat makes you gain ten pounds or more, guess again. It is not food but the thoughts that you place within the food that gives the food power over you. This "power" is an illusion.

We decide to be weak. We decide to give our Power over to something inanimate, valueless and give it meaning. Food is powerless. We do not want to take credit for our thoughts as having created our physical condition. We would rather believe our body controls us, that our body can use us to do things, and that our body can think.

Nothing in our body can think, neither bones, blood cells, muscles, tissues, molecules nor atoms. But they do have a consciousness, which is aligned with our Creator. You direct all your healthy or unhealthy condition by believing that something external to yourself is the cause for your unhappiness, your weight problem, money problem, or social relationships. The only thing your body does is respond to your thoughts.

Our body does respond to our love, or our condemnation. Our cells have a consciousness of life, energy and light because they come from Consciousness and Light and that is what they respond to, Energy.

The thoughts we hold onto manifest what we believe to be true about food. Our relationship with food is very powerful. Our thoughts have the power to bring negative results or positive results. Positive results would stem from the thoughts; "I never gain excess weight no matter what I eat", or "I am indifferent to food. I am no longer have the need to fear bread, ice cream or donuts. Everything I eat is light and filled with energy and is Holy. I charge all that I eat with the Presence of I Am before I eat it thereby rebuking any negative thought that may try to be a welcomed guest of mine at the table that God has created for me."

If you believe that anything can make you fat or can upset your stomach then you are right, in the world of illusion, but you are deceiving yourself. Your thoughts of littleness or weakness cause you to feel powerless with food, men, women, work and health.

You are not powerless unless you choose to be, unless you want to prove to yourself that you are weak and separated from God. Then you are powerless in your sight only, not in God's. "You are the thinker," as Phil Laut says in his book, **Money is My Friend**, "and your subconscious mind is the prover. It proves everything you believe to be true whether it is or not so that you won't go insane finding out that what you believe to be true is not. It does not decide for you what is true or not, but only has the job of bringing proof to you."

Refuse To Get Any Larger!

Have you ever asked yourself why it is that you've told yourself you won't go over a certain weight and then do or don't? I have had men and women say, "I've gone from a size 5-7, 9-10, 32-36 and I refuse to get any bigger!" Their prover (the universe, subconscious mind) has been instructed because of the strong desire in the thinker, to make sure the person does not get any larger than the stated size or weight. For those who have complained to me, 'I keep getting fatter, I keep gaining weight no matter what I do', the prover has been instructed by the thinker to provide 'truth' to the thinker and so, it is done.

Whatever we state with our spoken word (our thoughts with feeling) is what will be supplied to us without judgment from the universe even if it's good, right, or wrong for us. All IT does is fulfill our needs that we have requested of IT.

If you were to designate a desired weight, an ideal weight for yourself and believed and affirmed that you are that weight now, regardless of how you feel, or appear, you would soon be drawing unto you all the ways to fulfill that invisible substance to you to meet your faith. God who knows all our needs before we ask already meets all our desires.

We have to believe and accept our desires in the invisible plane first as though they were already present for our eyes to see on the visible plane; then we shall witness the manifestation of our belief.

"I Cannot Be Deceived"

God has already provided you with the consciousness for your desired weight and the ideal weight where you will feel good about yourself. All that is left for you to do is raise your consciousness to the level of having in the present, rather than I will have, or I am going to have. Take yourself out of the future and place yourself in the here and NOW.

Here are some examples of statements you can use below:

- I AM now in the Presence of you, Father.
- I AM now in the Presence of my ideal weight.
- I AM One with you Father. Thank you for your Love!

You do not have to beg or plead with God, convince, struggle or do anything but relax and release old ways of erroneous thoughts and allow God. **Be grateful** at all times! I repeat, **BE GRATEFUL at ALL TIMES**! Write out how grateful you are that you can now see the thoughts you have held that have kept you back from reaching your goals.

Talk out loud to yourself and to God about how glad you are to be able to wear all the things you have been saving to wear once you got back to your regular size. Write affirmations about how light and empty you feel now and how much slimmer you are and feel.

One of the greatest things I have learned from studying the Course is that "God is with me, I cannot be deceived." I cannot be deceived by my thoughts about situations, about people, about food or about myself ever again.

I now know:

- All food I eat is easily assimilated, metabolized and eliminated easily and effortlessly.
- All food I eat turns to health, beauty and slenderness.
- When I bless my food, my food blesses me in return with cosmic rays of light and raises the vibrations to that of Holiness not something to curse me or condemn me.
- If I condemn any food, it will condemn me in return because of the thoughts I just placed upon it, my false beliefs about it.
- If I bless my water and food then my holiness envelops it and I am protected from my own mis-creations.
- I know also that by blessing my food, my husband, children, I am enveloping them in my holiness and their holiness blesses and cares for me too.

Blessing and forgiving frees me from guilt, anger, hatred, separateness and the chains that would bind my spirit and mind to illusions and misperceptions in this world. Right-mindedness frees me to see without fear. It will free you too to begin accepting yourself and celebrating yourself.

I Am A Child Of The Absolute Good

Here is a game I made up which I shall share with you. See how many things during the day you can bless with your holiness. Write them down, or say out loud even as you pass a stranger. When you do this, you will find how happy it makes you, especially when you know what you are doing and know no one else knows that you are blessing her. Then you'll begin to realize that someone, perhaps a stranger from long ago, must have done the same to you without your knowing he or she was doing the same for you and having as much fun as you are now!

Establish the consciousness that "I am a child of the absolute Good. God is Good and I am Good. Everything that comes into my life is good, and so I am going to have only the good. Only the good is attracted to me and my life is in a perpetual state of joy!"
Emmett Fox writes, "We cannot ask for more substance from the universe for the universe is full of it, but we should rather ask for understanding to lay hold of it with our minds."

I want to say, know with your being that "I Am living in the peace of God. My lungs are breathing in the peace of God. My eyes are seeing with the Peace of God." Know this is because it is true. You are and never are not in the PRESENCE of God, because God is all, everything, in every place down to the subatomic particles of your cells. You are a cell of His Beingness; you are His Attribute in the flesh.

In the commandment that says, "Thou shall have no other gods before me!", it means do not give power to anything else. Do not separate yourself from the Truth of your being; do not worship fear, lack, anger, hate, lust or any other type of idol.

When your mind is relaxing in the Peace and Presence of God then you have the Power of God. Your heart will be healed in the Presence and Peace of God. Realize there is no conflict in God so there can be no conflict in you. Love your body and be grateful for it. As soon as you start loving your body, your cells will start to rejoice, rejuvenate, regenerate, and resurrect because of the Light and

Love energy you are allowing to become unblocked in your various chakra centers.

I Choose To Remember

Are you someone who always says, "I can't remember to do this or that like my wife or boss asks me to"? If you are, you are perpetuating that mind set to not allow yourself to move from that mind set. You can make the choice, the choice to start saying, "I can remember to do this and anything else if I choose. I choose to remember."

If the other hand, are you the wife or husband or boss who says, "He never remembers to do a single thing I ask him to do."? Maybe you could begin to start "knowing" that your employee, husband, wife or daughter is always cooperating with you in all you ask. State, "My husband is now removing all blockages from his mind that keep him from remembering. I am changing my perception of him and what he is capable of." You will begin to notice your perception of him/her changing from one of negative support to one of positive support in your thoughts. He will definitely notice it and become that which you now see in him. Your changed perception will literally lift him up.

Solutions come with the problems. They will be given to both of you from the invisible realm your egos could never have imagined existed before. Things will be made plain as day and you will laugh and say why didn't I think of this before.

Keep a spiritual journal. Write down the changes that you would like to see take place for yourself. Draw stick figures of all those involved and write the words you feel are appropriate in captions surrounded by a balloon above the heads.

Examples:

- My wife never helps with balancing of the checkbook.
- My wife now knows how to balance the checkbook and chooses to cooperate with me freely.
- I enjoy showing my wife how to do it.

- I forgive my wife for not knowing how to balance our checkbook. She is free and so am I. It is no longer important to me that she balances the checkbook.

If you find yourself always fussing and fuming over some 'little' thing, why not try doing and thinking the opposite and you will begin to live in a way you won't have to fuss and stew and fume over something which you cannot seem to be in control.

Examples:

- Mom is always saying loving things to me and doing loving things for me.
- I am always doing loving things for Mom, my wife, my friend.

There will always be people who will challenge that which we believe is the "norm" because they believe there are no limitations, except those that we place upon ourselves.

We are endowed with Christ consciousness. It enables us to speak, know, and do what mortal mind (surface mind) tells us we cannot do. Our Christ consciousness knows that we need only ask that there be Light on a situation and let it loose, let it go, and IT IS DONE!

I had a call from a friend and former Reiki Graduate of our Center. She said, "Daya, I have quite a story to tell you." I must preface this story by telling you that all my students are shown how to call forth the White Light of Protection around themselves, situations, their loved ones and vehicles. *(See Glossary)*

She told me she and her daughter Shannon had gone to visit a friend over in Ormond Beach, FL. It was the day of the full moon. She did not want to stay past sunset because she knows people can be strongly affected by the energy of the moon's vibrations in a powerfully negative way. She said that she knows from experience how drivers can and do weird things on the road. She did not want to drive on I-4 or I-95 so she asked her friend if there was a way to use a back road to get home. She was given directions but she did not write them down. She said she put the White Light of protection around her daughter, her car and herself and then they both left.

As she was driving, she noticed she was coming upon an intersection where she thought she needed to turn left. She got in the left-hand lane and then realized this might not be the turn she needed to make so she tried to get back into the right hand lane. There was a woman driver in that lane so she could not move over. Her daughter said, "Mom you can get over there now, you can try it." Patti told her No, I'll just go here and turn around if it's not the right street.

Patti's light turned green for the turn and as she was doing so, she noticed in her rearview mirror that a driver was racing down the middle of the street with a police car in hot pursuit. The light for the lane going straight turned green. As the woman started crossing the intersection, the car in pursuit hit her tail end. Patti's fingers gripped the steering wheel of her car as she gave thanks that she had listened about putting the White Light of Protection around her and her daughter. She asked and it was given her. It turns out that the left turn was in fact the right turn for her. She said, "Daya, I told Shannon, All we need to do is ask. It's there, all we have to do is ask."

Patti also shared that at one time she had a $4,000 hospital bill. Being a single parent this was something she could not afford to have hanging over her. She told me she prayed this prayer, "Dear God, take this from me. I deserve to be helped so I am giving it to you." She told me that $3,000 was written off completely, that of a $500 doctor bill, she only had to pay $91! She said, "You just have to release it! You just have to believe!"

If you allow God's Word to abide in you and Him in you, there is nothing you can ask and it shall not be given you. If what you ask is selfish, and goes against Law of Mind, which is cause and effect, seeing a manifestation of your prayer will not take place. You have to be willing to change your thinking and repent from that way of thought which put you in the situation from which you desire to be free.

You have to be grateful to God for what you have learned from the situation, problem or person. You have to be willing to release your hold of the situation in your mind, let it go, be willing to forgive the problem and loose it in Love.

All things in our lives are teachers. They teach us about patience, loving, giving, unselfishness and being judgmental, greed, lust, jealousy and more.

We have to be grateful for everything we are learning because it is putting us closer to knowing our Oneness with God. To know what pure joy and happiness really are, we must experience what it is like not to worry, not to have hateful feelings towards our brothers and sisters, but to have love and kindness towards them.

Many of my clients have said at one time or another that they hate their father, mother, sister, brother, aunt or someone in their family. They were not happy about the hatred they felt within. They wanted to get out of the cycle but didn't know how to be removed from the energy that was causing them so much pain.

Everyone wants to be loved, wants to love without conditions, and wants their love to be received. It brings tears to their hearts that they are not allowed to have their love received by another human being. But this is only true on a certain level of appearance. In the inner realm, you can surround that person with Light and Love and it will reach into their subconscious level. You can forgive them for what you perceive that they have done wrong to you.

You can do it in their presence or 1,000 miles away. It will still be received and accepted by their Higher Self. Whatever you send out into the universe is acted upon according to your feelings behind that thought.

What happens when we start acting and thinking in the present? The very thing desired will plop right down into our lap while we are not looking because we believed it to be so. You must remember, though that you cannot force your will upon anybody else just as God cannot force His Will upon you.

God can and does guide you through the Holy Spirit (His Executive Will) to bring you back to your remembrance of ONENESS with HIM.

All things are easy when we remember we are not the doers but God is. Our responsibility is to relax, let go and let God. We have to have faith in the Holy Spirit to correct our mistaken thoughts about the situation. We do this by inviting the Holy Spirit to correct our error thoughts and re-interpret them for us into TRUTH. What you can call for is a harmonious conclusion for all concerned and know that it shall be so.

Think of the situations in your life that you would like to change and then draw a funny situation below using stick figures and balloon captions. Place in the balloons the words you would like to see yourself saying or what you would like to see others saying to you. The result? - it works better than you could imagine.

Examples:

- Husband taking tissues out of his pockets before the clothes get put in the hamper so that lint won't be all over the other clothes when they are dried.
- Husband/wife helping with chores, baby, finances, hobby, vocation or whatever is relevant to you. Then release yourself from your expected outcome.

Look at the drawing everyday. Implant the reality of that happening by reading the words out loud. Feel it happening. Be thankful, grateful and let go. Allow God to answer your prayer. Allow yourself to trust that God KNOWS what is best for you. Trust for the first time. God is not like mortal mind, mortal man. God is Unlimited!

You may not want to believe this next statement, but it's true. No one is accountable for your thoughts and their effect upon you, except you; not God, not Jesus Christ, not your wife or husband, neighbor or friend. No one is responsible for your reaction to the things about you except you. You are the Master of your own thoughts, or the slave to your own thoughts.

According to the text of the Course, "Jesus cannot change your way of thinking because that would go against the LAW of MIND of cause and effect and interfere with your will, so you cannot plead with Jesus to help you on that level. You can ask Him to help you change your perception, your awareness and this He will do, but you have to be willing to accept His help after you have asked for it."

Whenever you want things to be a certain way for you, you are wishing, believing that if it could only happen. This is believing in doubt, and doubt only has the power to keep you from knowing your desire. But if you have faith, (which you do, but in the wrong direction at the moment) you'd say something like:

Example:

- I am thankful I can see it in a different way.

You would know the situation is now in the realm of God and you are in the realm of the NOW.

How To Stop Being Your Own Stumbling Block

Do you find yourself jealous of what someone else seems to have more of, or jealous of how they appear to look, feeling you lack the same and wish you could have it too? You already do have everything they have, except the consciousness as yet, but it is your gift from God as well.

We can have the consciousness of lack or the consciousness of abundance. It is our choice to choose what we believe in, what we want to place our faith in. Every one of us has been endowed with the Holy Spirit's Voice within us. It is available every second of our lives to re-interpret our fears of lack of health, lack of money, lack of love, or friends, if we but invite Him. Taking a **Super Vita-Mind** caplet here can dissolve all those stumbling blocks.

"Nothing Can Harm You"

When you use a dosage of **Super Vita-Minds**, you will find that nothing outside of yourself can injure you. Your fears are what create havoc in your life, not anyone or anything else. In reality, nothing can harm you. Fears are nothing-ness. Nothingness is nothing. Fears have no power but what you give to them. If you want to proclaim yourself as weak and your fears as strong, then you have free will do to do so.

You can change the thoughts you wish to hold in your mind just as easily as you have chosen to hold onto the fear thoughts you selected and believed you had to hold onto.

I counseled a young teenager who was proclaiming how much she hated her parents. I showed her how much more energy it takes to try to remember how much she hated her parents and all the mean things she thought they did to her. To be forgiving and loving towards them felt much better. She realized there was no pain or struggle to love and that she had to do absolutely nothing to remember she loved her parents, when she chose to be forgiving.

You may have selectively chosen to see your mother as unreasonable, abusive and unloving. You may have chosen to see your father, wife, brother, sister or husband as being untrustworthy, unreliable, hurtful and not capable of being loved.

You have selected to see whatever it is that makes you miserable and focus on it. You have also made up the reasons or justifications in your mind as to why you had to believe you hated them. But you can choose to see with the eyes of Christ because you are one with Christ.

Each one of us is the Father, Son and Holy Spirit. Each one of us has the same Christ consciousness as Jesus has. This enlightened consciousness tells us that the Father and I are One. Each one of us is the Mind, Idea and Action. God being Mind, Jesus Christ being the Idea and the Holy Spirit the Action the Law Bearer or Executive of the Will of God. You have the tools you need to change how you "look" at what you see. When you choose to see beyond your ego's perception of separation, you will see that you are ONE with your sister, ONE with Mind and that it is not possible to hate as you were told you had to do." (*See References,* **Dabney's Handbook on A Course in Miracles**).

Be willing to believe, "I **can** love myself today!"

Brief Points of Chapter

- You can dissolve negative conditions in your life.
- You can experience living in the present.
- How to look at situations differently.
- Techniques to use to become unblocked.
- How to let go and let God do the work necessary for you.
- How to stop being your own stumbling block.

Ringlets of Laughter

Press your heart to my heart.
Feel the molecules of joy
Pass across our invisible bond of light
Gathering moonbeams, ringlets of laughter,
And cosmic rays
Feel the fairies tinkling their feet in
The Raining, sprinkling stardust
that fills the
Bowls of our hearts as we laugh
and laugh and laugh.

Daya Devi-Doolin,
Returning to the Source

CHAPTER FOUR

THE LAW OF CAUSE AND EFFECT

How To Co-Create With God

We are co-creators with God. Being a co-creator with God is our natural state of being. You are One with Him regardless of how long in time it takes for you to remember and believe this. You are the THOUGHT of God. In your at-one-ment with God you can create all that is good or holy. It means you are not unplugged from your source of life.

You can create love, forgiveness, wholeness, and miracles in your life because you are these things already. It's when we forget we are not separate from God that we begin to mis-create. Co-creating is no longer living in the world of illusion and believing in it. The world of death, age, loss and lack is over.

As co-creators, we have dominion over our thoughts. Our thoughts are the cause which lead to the effect of what appears in our world. It is no one's responsibility but ours for the cause and the effect of our thoughts. It is only we ourselves who can say, "I Am." No one else can do that for us.

What our attention is on, we draw unto us or become. Our attention to a thing, person or condition puts our life energy into it. We draw that quality to ourselves from the invisible to our visible realm, mirroring what we focused on. It can be positive or negative.

What we focus on with our I AM consciousness is what we draw into our world. This is the Law of Cause and Effect. It is the law. Jesus said, "I of Myself can do nothing, it is the Father within Me that doeth the works." He was recognizing the individualized God Presence, the I AM THAT I AM. It was not ego that was the doer, but God.

As explained in A. D. Luk's books, **The Law of Life Vol. I and II**, "The law of cause and effect is the law, the law of energy and vibration. The law is not someone's opinion, concept or theory but law, universal and cosmic which is impersonal that never did and cannot fail. The law works because of the feelings you put behind the word or thought and it releases currents from your I AM Presence which produces the manifestation."

If you say, "Well, I have spoken affirmations and denial statements and the law does not work." It has not worked because there has been some doubt in your consciousness and you put more faith and feeling in your doubt than you did in the desired end. Putting your faith in doubt enabled you to put other gods before you.

You are the law. You are the I AM Presence. You alone can call on your Presence to act for you, no one else can. A.D. Luk says, "The I AM Presence is the all pervading principle in life, the most divine activity in the universe. It is the only active principle each one of us has. It is ever striving for expression to produce perfection through each of us. I AM is the life principle in your body. It is the principle of life expressed through Jesus Christ. I AM is the creative word, the initial word that produced creation and from which all creation springs. The words I AM are the two cups that carry the power into outer activity. The use of the word I AM denotes individualized being."

When you invoke the words I AM, you are calling forth life into manifestation. It releases energy from your God source and it becomes manifest in your life.

If you are wondering as many of us have, why is my life this way or that and why can't I do anything about it to change it? The answer is you can, and only you can. You have made up certain erroneous laws about life and *your* life, which you are soon to discover if you do not know already. If you are ready, we can begin to discard those old laws, archaic tapes and replace them with Law of Mind.

I myself wanted to know what laws had I made that put me in the physical shape I was in (thought I was in, that of being overweight). When I was nineteen years old, I was five pounds overweight and decided that was too much. I had made up my law, which was unreasonable, so I had to become dissatisfied with myself because of my rule.

I wrote the laws down which attracted my overweight problem to me. I had claimed it as my problem. They are listed below:

- I don't listen to the Holy Spirit's guidance.
- I don't like my stomach or abdomen so I perpetuate my weight problem by not liking it (putting all my feeling energy into the hate and putting other gods before me); therefore my body had to keep itself in a state of that consciousness. Now I could continually prove to myself what I "believed" was right, regardless of whether it was a lie.
- I believe food is "fattening". I believe I am guilty for eating and I believe I harm myself by the foods I eat. Rather than know all food comes from God and therefore no food is harmful to me except what fears I place upon it, I pretend to know what God is feeling while I live in my own ego consciousness world.
- I do not eat when I am hungry and I do not stop when the Holy Spirit tells me that I am full. I hear when I am full, but I ignore it and give myself excuses why I can't waste the food. I won't be good if I leave food on my plate. I do not realize that I can save it for a later day or even eat it only when I am hungry. The

next process I had to undergo, in order to learn what laws I had made for myself that were not making me happy was to list the fears I had of letting go of the laws. What would I be losing if I gave up the problem?

- I have made myself believe that I am unworthy of good according to past relative's perception of me; so I had to prove to myself I was not worthy to live up to my expectations. I merely accepted those that were projected onto me. I did not know I could choose not to accept anyone's beliefs about me that were incorrect.
- Now I know I am worthy of all good. I Am the Good in all things. I am Holy and every cell, nerve and fiber in me is Holy and knows it has the consciousness of Holiness.
- I am afraid I'll be a failure at releasing weight, therefore since I am afraid, that consciousness of fear keeps me in failure because of the energy I put into that false belief about myself. I always have to do what I believe even if it is false or negative because it proves me right. When I get out of the fear consciousness, by my choice, I'll know that nothing can cause me to be afraid. I will know I am invulnerable as a child of God, to any fearful thoughts.
- I keep saying to myself, "It's hopeless" instead of "It's hopeful." That consciousness of lack keeps me hopeless and fulfills my false image about myself. I am now full of hope. I AM HOPE!
- I trust my heart.
- I trust my heart.
- I trust my heart.
- I trust my heart.
- I trust my heart.

I felt the need to write these many times until I finally believed it and felt good about it. Perhaps you may find you will need to do this or something similar as Spirit leads you.

I also wrote:

- I, Daya, am now willing for my beauty to come forth and I am now willing for everyone to like me including people of my past, present and future.

- I, Daya the Christ, AM one with God. It is safe for me to be my ideal weight and be pregnant too.

- I, Daya, the Christ, can and do eat anything I want without feeling unhappy, guilty or shameful and no longer give my power to powerless food.

- I, Daya, the Christ, love myself for eating whatever makes me happy no matter what it is. I choose to be happy about all things without being attached to it.

- I, Daya, choose to eat only when I am absolutely hungry and choose to stop before I am full.

One of the things that was revealed to me by God is, "You are to forgive all your wrong thinking and give it all over to the Holy Spirit. Be at peace with yourself and know you are not alone. You are not as you think you are. Love dwells within you because you are Love created like Itself. Live in the now. Share loving, the gift I give to you. Give up your false beliefs, the ones that say you are in control."

I needed to know which steps to take to apply this to my life and so I was given some applications or blueprints for knowing, which are:

Application and Blueprint for Knowing:

- Know that I AM ONE with God.
- Bring your bitterness to the Holy Spirit.
- Forgive who you think you are.

Then I had to write:

- I, Daya, being the Christ, feel safe and have no fear of giving up illusions or my "weight" problem.
- I, Daya, being the Christ am willing for others to see how attractive I really am. I no longer feel ashamed.
- I, Daya, being the Christ am without imperfection for I am attractive.
- It's OK for me to show others I am not afraid of myself or life.
- I don't have to hide my beauty like I was made to believe by a deceased relative.
- I forgive her for her misperceptions about me. I release her in Love and thank her for the teacher she has been to me.
- I, Daya, being the Christ, am now satisfied with myself, my weight, my life and I praise God everyday that I can praise Him for the gift of gratitude and all that it brings. I am thankful to have found out that I had been ungrateful for my increase in body weight, and that I was never satisfied when I was slender.

From one of the lessons in the workbook of the Course, God's law is that "I cannot be deceived." I decided to find out what my laws were that tried to refute His Law in my life. What was it that puffed me up to be greater than He?

The *Answer*:

> My law is that I believe I Am overweight, so I am because I made up that law for myself. It manifested my truth for me to prove me right, to prove I am God.

> But I made myself unhappy by this truth just so I could be right. God's law is, I am my perfect ideal weight right now, underneath my illusion. Problem solved!

My second law was discovered to be:

> I can't see without my glasses. All my faith is in believing I need glasses. I have not surrendered them to God or trusted enough to know I can see perfectly well without them. I have rather believed in my family's and doctor's viewpoint of truth for me.

My third law was:

> I am not perfect. But that doesn't mean anything if it doesn't make me happy. None of my laws are capable of doing so unless my Will is God's Will.

What laws have you made up for yourself to believe in and prove yourself right, though unhappy? Is it that your skin is the wrong shade, color, your face is the wrong shape, your eyes are too small, too big, too wide apart, too narrow, too ugly, the wrong color, your body the wrong shape. Has your law said you are too thin, too muscular, too flabby and too heavy?

Take a moment right now and write down in your journal the laws you have made up for yourself which may or may not be true. You can choose to change your laws, your thoughts about yourself and begin by knowing God's law is that you cannot be deceived. If you choose to believe in your laws, you are choosing to be deceived temporarily and choosing to be unhappy about all your affairs at the same time.

Here is a list of some other laws you may have chosen to believe in which have not made you happy. Check off which ones apply to you and write them in the back of the book on the journal pages.

- I am lonely.
- I am an alcoholic.
- I am alone, deserted, fearful.

- I am getting old.
- I am too old.
- Everything I eat is bad for me.
- Water is unsafe for me to drink.
- I never have enough money.
- I am always sick.
- I don't have any friends.
- I can't trust my husband, wife.
- I can't have children.
- Nobody loves me.
- I am all alone.
- I am in pain.
- I have cancer, arthritis, FIBROMYALGIA, CFS, MS.
- I am ADD/ADHD child/adult.
- I am manic-depressive.
- I cannot trust anyone.
- Life is a struggle. I can never get ahead.
- I have an obsessive-compulsive behavior.

But God's laws are and remain and He wants us to know:

- You are not lonely.
- You are not alone for Christ is with you even now and always has been.
- You are immortal, eternal and beautiful.
- Everything I give you is Holy.
- You are Abundance.
- You are Whole and Well at all times.
- I Love You.

The laws brought about by ego keep you where you know you don't want to be. But your desire to remain in that level of energy consciousness can do nothing except prove to you that you are right about your laws, even though you are unhappy in them.

How To Tap Into His Abundance

God's abundance is all around us, as soon as we raise our level of thoughts to thoughts of His Oneness with us. His abundance, His Divine Substance is and always has been waiting for us to accept and receive.

Everything you truly want and desire like love, wisdom, power, abundance, prosperity, strength, light/energy aliveness, joy, all await you when you surrender your laws, totally and completely to Him. Then, you accept His laws which say, You Cannot Be Deceived Because I Love You! The desire you have in your heart to be free of the mind trap you feel you are in is His desire in you, so that you can come to know and trust Him when you have forsaken your "self."

Circle some of your laws.

I am afraid of growing older.	There is nothing to fear.
I am afraid of doctors.	There is nothing to fear.
I am afraid of needles.	There is nothing to fear.
I am afraid of hospitals.	There is nothing to fear.
I am afraid of money.	There is nothing to fear.
I am afraid of being poor.	There is nothing to fear.
I am afraid of food.	There is nothing to fear.
I am afraid of my parents.	There is nothing to fear.
I am afraid to love my parents.	There is nothing to fear.
I am afraid for my children.	There is nothing to fear.
I am afraid to give up my fears.	There is nothing to fear.
I am afraid I am not a good friend.	There is nothing to fear.
I am afraid to attend church.	There is nothing to fear.
I am afraid to reveal my desires.	There is nothing to fear.
I am afraid to express my ideas	There is nothing to fear.
I am afraid I am different.	There is nothing to fear.
I am afraid to try things.	There is nothing to fear.

If any of these laws or others exist for you now, cross them off and replace them gently with God's law from the Course that,

"There is nothing to fear." My laws are unreal. They do not exist. My laws are now God's laws, for I AM ONE with God.

As you cross off these laws of yours, say aloud to yourself, or watch yourself say it in front of your mirror, I am no longer afraid of me anymore. Watch the feelings of joy well up inside your heart so fast that you feel the joy wants to jump outside of you. Say, "I surrender all my past, present and future illusions, laws and fears to the Holy Spirit."

How To Cancel Out Mis-Beliefs

Now you can know you have nothing to fear. You made up your own fears and you can unmake them up in your mind so that you too can know the peace, joy and happiness there is for you to know. Otherwise, you would not desire to know happiness.

You see happiness in other people and you wonder how can I know that same happiness that they seem to know. You can know it by giving yourself a dose of **Super Vita-Minds** to freely release all your fears and laws to God and rest in His Love.

Some of the things you can now know are:

- I trust you Father.
- I rest in you Father.
- I love you Father.
- Thank you for loving me.
- I am One with You.

When you release your fears into God's Hands, what you are doing is giving up or withdrawing your faith in your laws, and investing your faith in what is TRUTH. When you perceive truly, you will be cancelling out mis-beliefs in yourself, in others and in the world around you.

After reading chapter two in the text of the Course, I asked the Holy Spirit to help me understand how to apply the lesson to my life. This is the channeled information that I received as my answer.

"Love is not insane, but ego would have you believe that it is insane not to be insane. Ego wants you to believe that miracles are pills, money, illness and death which you need to be happy. Ego would keep you separate from knowing who you really are and believe that the natural order of things is seen as "miracles" through ego's eyes. Ego projects its own meaning onto what it sees and gives false security in its meaning. The voice is louder and more fearful in order to try to drown out the sound of MY VOICE. But MY VOICE is never forgotten. You may choose to turn down the volume or bypass it, but it shall never be apart from you.

> You are MY VOICE. Once you allow your miracles to be put in their perspective, you will know what is a miracle. Miracles are Love manifest and it cannot be not manifested. Love is the natural order of all things and is never absent. Miracles cannot be greater or lesser. They are waiting to manifest behind everything that obscures Love.
>
> Being blind does not mean that miracles do not exist or are missing. Peace and miracles are always present, you have to uncover them by being receptive to MY Peace, by being forgiving."

I was then given these affirmations on how to apply this knowing to my life:

- I AM ONE with miracles.
- Expect only what is natural.
- Forgiveness is the miracle.

After reading chapter three of the Course, I wanted to receive from Spirit answers on how to look beyond my illusions, my laws. Chapter three was about Innocence and Perception.

I was told by Spirit:

> "Innocence as you know it is pure in behavior and thought. Ego as you made it is deceptive only to preserve itself and keep the truth about yourself from your SELF. It "squawks" loudly so as to distract you from hearing My Voice. Perception frees you from questioning, as only ego knows how to do much of.

> Ego knows only questions because it knows it cannot know, or answer. It knows how to keep you occupied with questions so you won't hear the answers."

I was given this blueprint for applying to my life:

- Rise above the ego's voice, or lift your mind above ego's voice.
- Look beyond the questions.
- Look beyond illusions.
- Be still - know you are one with your SELF, One With Me.

Your Affirmations:

- Everyday, I become One with the Word of God.
- I am exhausting limited self and expanding my awareness of my limitlessness.
- Knowledge is always by my side.
- Each minute brings me closer to shedding my ego and replacing it with knowledge.
- I listen to Your Voice and I am free.
- The puddle I now see will expand into a huge looking glass reflecting back to me the love I see in others.
- A watchful eye always knows that which the ego is trying to hide.

You, your ego self, does not wish change. It does not want anything unfamiliar into its life unless it puts it there. It is nothing. It wants to feel weak, afraid, sick and penniless to get sympathy and to try to be the vengeful punisher for God as it feels He would punish us. God does not punish. God is not vengeful. God does not forgive us for there is not anything that we have done to be forgiven for. We have to forgive ourselves and others for the gift it brings us, the freedom from being bound to another in a negative way.

Giving up our laws may seem hard, but once you taste the joy of giving up and surrendering, you will never turn back, you won't be able to. You will have passed through the door of everything beyond the unreal door of ego. You can read more about this in Dorothy Ruby's book, **The Door of Everything.** (*See Reference*).

How To Determine What Your Ego Is Like

Here are some exercises that have been very helpful to many of my students.

- Draw a picture of yourself as you think others see you. Draw one of yourself as you see yourself and the third, as you think God sees you.
- Make a list of the errors you see in others.
- Make a list of the truths you see in them. (i.e. I judge all things as I would have them be).
- Make a list of the errors you see in yourself.
- What specific areas of errors do you focus on seeing in another person when you first see or meet them.
- What are the truth areas you focus on first?
- I now forgive myself and others for all the errors I perceived him/her to have or be or do.
- Affirmation to repeat to yourself over and over and over, "He or She is the Living Christ and so am I."
- Who is the one person you hate most in the world right this moment? Now say to yourself aloud, I see the Living Christ in ________________, And So It Is!

After reading chapter five in **ACIM**, I asked that I be given a summary for a better understanding. My request was granted as always and it is included below:

- You are to forgive all your wrong thinking and give it all over to the Holy Spirit.

- Be at peace with yourself and know you are not alone. You are not as you think you are.
- Love dwells within you because you are Love created like Itself.
- Live in the now. Share loving, the gift I give to you.
- Give up your false beliefs, the ones that say you are in control.

The applications for knowing and for following this channeled information are below:

- Know that I AM ONE.
- Bring your bitterness to the Holy Spirit.
- Forgive who you think you are.

Brief Points of Chapter

- The Law of cause and effect makes your reality.
- What to do to tap into God's abundance.
- How to cancel out your mis-beliefs about yourself.
- How to determine what your ego is like.

Waterfall Wonder

Does a waterfall wonder
If it knows how to fall?
Does it hurt itself
On the way down?
Does it wonder if fish
Will slip from its grip;
Or if rocks will be there when it falls?
Will there be enough water
To land just right
Or to move at its regular pace?
I wonder if I wonder too much
And does it wonder at all.
I think it probably knows what's best
And doesn't wonder at all.

Daya Devi-Doolin

CHAPTER FIVE

SUPER VITA-MINDS

ENERGIZED THOUGHT FORMS

Thought Forms

I know that changing your mind, your attitude does not happen overnight and you should not feel less than perfect when that does not happen in 30 seconds! It's possible for it to happen, don't get me wrong, but you have to really have deep faith and commitment for it to occur for yourself.

Spirit gave the title, **Super Vita-Minds**, to me for a book that I would write. It means energized thought forms that charge your energy field, that make you feel alive, alert, loving and forgiving with each daily dosage. They replace the old debilitating thought forms that you collected so long ago that never worked. You kept your faith in them until they proved that they could no longer serve you for your good. **Super Vita-Minds,** invigorate your energy field and make you glow.

These thought forms are encapsulated and highly vibrational because they are vibrating with Christ-Mind qualities, the Mind that Jesus said that we could call upon at anytime.

Forty-Day Program

You will find, in this chapter, **Super Vita-Minds** that you can use for the next 40 days. You can also use just one for 40 days and experience the joy that follows and engulfs you each and every second. People will start asking you, "What are you smiling about all the time?" They'll be wondering if you are laughing at them for some reason or other. They will not be able to understand a person can be joyful without being joyful about attacking someone or condemning them.

Of course, those who know they are in tune will be in tune with you and will know why you are so joyous because they will recognize the Christ-ness in you, as in themselves.

Effortless Changes

If your concern is weight loss, you may find your diet will change automatically without any effort on your part. You'll look forward to eating and choosing foods differently. You won't be satisfied with your ordinary way of eating.

You may find during these next forty days that you love people more, unconditionally, even that mother-in-law whom you say now you absolutely hate. You may find a *lightness* about you that you cannot explain. That is because love is replacing darkness that was once hiding out in your cells, your tissues, your heart and soul. If you wish to extend it for longer period, I have included extra days for you.

Your Spiritual Journal

In the back of this book, you will find a section for a spiritual journal to keep track of your achievements during this period or any other goals that you have accomplished. I would also put any revelations or miracles that you have seen, received or experienced yourself. Mark the date on each page for later reference.

I would suggest that you take a dose of your **Super Vita-Minds** prescription before you get out of bed in the morning and before you close your eyes in the evening. Allow yourself to be quiet after you drink in the words. Feel the power that they generate within you. Look at the power they will generate in your entire body. Your body will tingle with the Holy Presence when you do because you have invited it.

Super Vita-Minds:

1. I breathe in the Peace of God.
2. I rest in the Peace of God.
3. I live in the Peace of God.
4. I love in the Peace of God.
5. I sleep in the Peace of God.
6. I am willing to and I intend to forgive my (sister, mother, father, the auto mechanic, doctor, surgeon, co-worker, supervisor, son, daughter, the rain, hurricane, God, the hit and run driver, minister, murderer).
7. I do forgive (any of the above, all of the above or insert your own situation). Note how you feel after you have said each word with feeling.
8. I want to know the cause of my "problem."
9. I know the cause of my "problem."
10. I want to surrender my problem to the Holy Spirit.
11. I am surrendering my problem to the Holy Spirit.
12. I have surrendered my problem to the Holy Spirit.
13. I know I do not have the responsibility of trying to solve anything. My responsibility is to be aware that all is well and to believe it.
14. I do not have to hate anymore. I give myself permission to love others and myself unconditionally.
15. I give myself permission to forgive myself for being (weak, non-goal-oriented, unloving, unforgiving, not

being there for my friend, my children, my husband, my wife, too fat, too skinny, too lustful, too jealous, too greedy, too selfish, too religious, not religious enough, etc.)

16. I no longer attach myself to the past. The past is not here, but I am. I am now and I am not alone.
17. Everyone loves me. It is their desire to prosper me and to help at anytime.
18. I love everyone. It is my desire to prosper everyone whom I can when called upon or not.
19. My breath is slow and quiet. Peace flows through me like a river.
20. All physical problems are dissolved along with my faith in them. I am thankful.
21. I can call for help from God and get an immediate answer because I am willing to receive His help. I know that God is my source, my supply and my health. I know that I AM GOD.
22. Ego can no longer tell me what to do. I am ego-less.
23. All my energy centers (chakras) are cleared and filled with Cosmic Light Rays. I am receiving light right now whether I believe it or not. I am Light whether I believe it or not. It is so!
24. If I <u>have</u> to smoke, or eat, or drink I invite the Holy Spirit to be with me, to lift me up from guilt thoughts, sadness, helplessness thoughts, anxiety thoughts, fear or worry thoughts. I decide with God in all my choices.
25. I no longer need to abuse anyone else or myself.
26. I am perfect in God-Mind. In ego mind I am not. I am nothing in ego's mind. In God-Mind I AM THAT I AM.
27. I am One with all my family members because we are from One-Mind. I do not have to try to get along with them. I do get along beautifully with them. Nothing is lacking in our relationship.

28. All my needs and desires are being abundantly supplied and manifested right now. I am Christ-consciousness and therefore I am supply, abundance, happiness, love and joy.
29. I am Whole.
30. I am certain I want to be Whole.
31. I am absolutely certain I am Whole.
32. I am the Knower of Everything.
33. I am Still.
34. Hatred and unforgiveness bring about disease, bodily ailments and all other kinds of pain and suffering. Why would I choose this instead of joy and happiness?
35. I am a child of God, a Holy child of God. No one is anymore or less than his brother/sister, therefore everyone is as Holy as I am.
36. Would I rather be at peace and happy all day long or would I rather spend time attacking my brother? The choice is always mine.
37. What brings me more joy, being loved or being hated?
38. Who do I think I am to condemn that which God has given me? I am made in His image, perfect, but not yet complete. I make myself unhappy when I choose to believe otherwise.
39. Love will not be seen today if I choose not to see it.
40. If I am unhappy it is because I have forgotten everything I have is Holy. So I remind myself I have: a Holy Spirit, a Holy body, Holy thoughts, Holy organs, muscles, arms, fingers, legs, eye, a Holy family, a Holy job, house to live-in, holy money and affairs.

If you would like to add more days to your program, please indulge yourself.

41. Only God who cannot create anything unlike Himself gave everything I have ever been given. I have much to be grateful for every day. If I don't, it's because I have chosen to think I have not received it.

42. Condemning my situation or myself is the best way to be sure I'll remain in it. I now choose to have my consciousness lifted to a new level, being grateful all the while. This is the best way to change what I desire to be changed in a twinkling.
43. Love is always with me because I am Love. Worry only makes my illusions real; release from them gives them no power.

Taking this encapsulated **Super Vita-Minds** for forty days will guarantee for you a clearing out of any unwanted negative mental energy, also known as erroneous thinking.

You may not be able to see the results immediately but that does not mean you have failed to effect a change within yourself. You will have made tremendous inroads. Just the desire alone has brought you closer and drawn unto you all the invisible help you could ever imagine. By invisible help I mean that help coming from the Holy Ascended Beings known as the Great White Brotherhood, Christ, and our Archangels, Michael, Rapheal, Zadkiel, Jopheil and the whole Host of Angelic Beings. They are the offspring of God as are we.

In our Father's kingdom, Jesus has told us, there are many mansions. This means there are many levels of consciousness that we can reach. His Voice is that which guides and leads and supports us through the action of the Holy Comforter in our hearts. When we are quiet, we hear that Oneness, feel that Oneness and become that Oneness. We are witnesses to the awesome beauty of it all.

Try placing your hands cupped over both ears. Now breathe deeply, letting your shoulders drop and relax. Lower your breath into your lower body. You will begin to hear the Holy Nod, called also the Holy Spirit. You will hear the sound of OM, a sound like a waterfall or the sound of the ocean kissing the beach and receding.

You can help yourself grow very quickly the more you invite the Holy Spirit to speak to you and guide you every day.

Decide To Enjoy Life

You know how you decide it is time to get rid of your old clothing, old articles of the past and throw them away. Well, think of your old habits, old ways of thinking about yourself as old clothes, not useful anymore because they don't fit. Decide that abusing yourself is no longer helpful, pleasing or satisfying for you to learn from. Decide that saying, "I am a loser", is no longer able to fit into your new level of awareness. It sticks out like a tear in a new garment. Decide that you are going to enjoy life.

I once heard William Shatner say in a interview how he was going to stop and smell the roses if it killed him despite any obstacles that tried to stop him from doing so. As he sniffed the rose he held close up to his nostrils he started laughing with gusto!

How To Decide To Be Happy

This is your life, your choice. Only you can make the difference in your life. You can say I hate you to yourself everyday of your life and it will never bring you the joy you know must be "out there". You can also say I deserve to be happy regardless of what I used to believe about myself or what anyone else believes is true about me now. I was wrong but I can change my beliefs about myself. I will change my belief. I will absorb my **Super Vita-Minds** capsules into my subconscious bloodstream and be uplifted. I do accept my Christ-ness. It is my inheritance from the universe. I intend to be happy now because I have decided to do so!

Brief Points of Chapter

- How to charge and change your energy field.
- How to change effortlessly with **Super Vita-Minds**.

- Make the decision to enjoy life.
- How to decide to be happy.

The Only Way Out

There is a peaceful path,
There is an inner way
To the eternal quest
All the sages say.

Seeker, turn within.
Seeker, turn without.
The Inner Light will make you win,
Just let go, let God, give in!

There is a peaceful path,
There is a way from fear.
This is the only way out
And that way is
Here.

Daya Devi-Doolin

CHAPTER SIX

HOW TO RELEASE YOURSELF FROM FEAR

How To "Get" Cancer

Do you want Cancer? Do you want any kind of disease? I know you are thinking, "What kind of stupid question is that? Why would anyone have to ask such a question? Nobody wants Cancer."

I ask it because people with whom I have counseled always feel they have no choice in the matter. They think that Cancer or any other illness is just sitting "out there", waiting to pounce on the fiftieth person that walks by a department store, a person, a hot dog stand or whatever. I hear people say things like, "I hope I don't get it. I don't know what I'd do if I got it", or, "I'm afraid to sit too long in the sun for fear I might get Cancer."

ALL THINGS, ALL SITUATIONS, ALL PEOPLE, ALL EXPERIENCES, COME TO US BY OUR CHOICE, BECAUSE WE HAVE SUMMONED THEM UNTO OURSELVES TO MAKE OUR REALITY REAL AND TO LEARN FROM THEM.

We have all been blessed with the power of our spoken word, our thoughts and the belief and faith we put behind our Word (thought). None of our thoughts are idle, or lie idle for that matter, for we are created in the likeness of God and are co-creators with God. We have the power to create or mis-create anything by claiming it so and so it shall be. That which we think is that which is. That is our inheritance.

Attracting Like Thought Forms

Similar thought forms are attracted by thoughts we send out. Thoughts vibrate at various hertz frequencies depending on how pure or impure the thought is. All thoughts either connect with positive life force or negative life force. This is how we create our world of illusion or reality. We can say we know what is happening and the other person does not. We now believe we are better than they.

I Do Not Believe

If you believe that diseases, misfortunes, catastrophes are out to get you, then you are giving up your God strength to ego-strength, which is powerlessness. You are believing that you are the body. You are saying, "I do not believe or know that I am as powerful as God made me." You are saying with arrogance, "I am right and God is not." You are saying, "God made me weak and I am going to prove myself right even if it kills me, or makes me unhappy, sick or miserable."

If you believe you are the body, then you are going to be playing right into the hands of ego. It has only one objective, to make you believe you are nothing but the body. Ego tells you that you are weak, infallible, susceptible and powerless to prevent any misfortune from coming your way, consuming you in despair and grief.

You Are Strong And All Powerful

What you are is Spirit, all powerful, all knowing, all Life because you are a son or daughter of God. Your body, your bones, your blood, your cells, your nerves, your muscles are all billions and billions of atoms, non-thinking atoms. They respond to your thought waves, thought vibrations, thought beliefs. As I have said in Chapter 1, your body cannot think. It represents what you think as evidenced by your radiance or lack of radiance in your eyes or presence.

The body cannot say, "I will lay here in bed today" and then do so. It cannot be sick, unless you tell it to be so or give it permission. If you command it to be sick but do not specify how, you will be sick in a way that you would not have imagined and wonder why this is now happening to you.

You do not expect the pain that comes along with your desire to be sick. Your body has no choice but to react willingly to your invocations of sickness. When you invoke the qualities of health and healing, immediately these life forms will be attracted to you to aid you. That's the rule of the universe, the Law of Spirit, the Law of Mind. Their roles are to offer unto us all that we desire if we believe strongly enough in our thoughts. That is why prayers are so powerful! They are affirmations of the truth about your being. They place you in the "now" of healing.

Who Are You?

You are Mind, as God is Mind. You are One with God so you are One with your Self. Your body has no choice but to do as the Mind has requested. A good reference book along these lines is, **Your Body Believes What You Say To It,** by Barbara Hoffman Levine. (*See References*). When your body is told with emotion to re-create itself, the sub-conscious mind goes about its job making sure all cells, atoms and sub-atomic particles do exactly what they are impressed to do.

How Does Error Thought Work?

When you put your faith in error thoughts which, for example, says, "My body tells me it's feeling sick", you do not want to take credit for your thoughts, which are mis-creating a sickness in the first place. You may have thought, "I sure would like to take a day off from work," but felt guilty doing so without being sick. You did not give yourself permission to be off from work without an excuse. It is okay to do so.

You did not feel you deserved to have a day off without a need to be ill to justify it, so you conjured up your cells together, to behave in a dis-harmonious manner. Your ego self will deny what I am saying and begin to feel angry towards me for even suggesting you would want to harm yourself. Please read this section again until you can *know* it.

You want to put the blame for the fibromyalgia, chronic fatigue syndrome and cancer onto some external thing, something external to yourself so you won't feel guilty about it or be responsible for your state of mind or predicament. You may even want to blame God for not hearing your prayer. You may even want to blame God for sending this awful plague upon you for no apparent reason.

All I Wanted Was A Little Sympathy

When you manage to get yourself sick, "incurably" so, you look for sympathy for your condition. People will feel sorry for you. So you will have control over them. They will remain with you tied only by sympathy. That is a heck of a way to get attention, to get yourself in agony for what? Just so you can hear, "Gee, I'm sorry this happened to you."

What does that really do for you? Does it get you well? Does it heal you? Does it re-organize all your atoms and molecules to their healthy state of being? No.

It does help you keep focusing on your own error thoughts, which created the condition in first place. It does keep you miserable.

Your ego self does not want to help you get out of the mental bind you are in, so you look for an external reason to be "carrying the cross", to punish yourself. Your ego self wants to say to God, "Look, I proved you wrong, and I am right. I am weak, not all-powerful. Even though I am not happy, not well, I Am right!"

Six Easy Steps To Get Cancer Or Any Other Disease

Becoming ill is very easy to do. Here are six easy steps to prove your error thoughts about yourself are right:

- Be fearful of everything (yourself, people, water, heights, germs, food, death, money). Do not breathe. Numb yourself from feeling.
- Hold the thought that all negative things that come to you are not due to your thoughts.
- Hold thoughts of resentment and bitterness for years and years and years in your energy field. Make sure that your cells are forced to give up their life force and be replaced by the negative waveform that resentment embraces.
- Believe that only you are right in all situations whether you are or not.
- Always be unforgiving towards nature, creatures, political figures, organizations, people that have different views from yours.
- Always be bitter, resentful and critical. Always be ungrateful to God, to Life, to the universe for your current mate, job, children, life, money or lack and limitation of any kind.

I believe that no one in her right mind would choose to be one with sickness or any other illusion once she remembers that she has a choice in choosing health over sickness or mental/emotional illnesses. I believe everyone wants to be well and to stay well, but you will have to work for it just as you worked hard to become ill.

You will have to change your attitude from one of helplessness to one of, "I Am Strong." You will have to know, "I have been given the gift of health, the knowledge of health, for I Am One with God." You will have to believe that, "I can know that I Am Light through and through. I can know that I, being Christ, Am the Truth, the Way and the Light. I can know all if all is forgiven and right with me."

Becoming well is just as easy as attracting sickness. Just reverse the six steps above to:

- I no longer fear anything, for "Nothing unreal exists", (**ACIM**) and cancer is unreal. I breathe fully. I choose to feel my emotions and release them.
- I offer all my mis-creations to the Holy Spirit and surrender all my attachments to them right now.
- I risk giving all thoughts of resentment and bitterness into the Hands of the Holy Spirit. I AM FREE.
- I choose only to be happy.
- I forgive everyone, everything, nature, God, organizations, the rapist, murderer, bill collector, nations, my mother and father and everyone and everything forgives me. I release them in love to the universe and thank them for the teacher they have been to me. They were teachers in order for me to learn about myself and draw me closer to my God awareness.
- I am always grateful to God. Every day I have 490 things to thank God for, to thank the universe for and to thank life for. I no longer condemn my body or anybody else. I am grateful to myself for loving myself. I give myself permission to love myself and to smile.

"You're Not Afraid To Fly?"

As I was travelling during a Christmas holiday, I was waiting for a flight in the airport lobby. There was a mother with her husband and toddler son waiting also. I first noticed them as they were talking to her father on the pay phone right next to me. They were wishing him a Merry Christmas and had coached the son to say "Hi", to Grandpa and to wish him a Merry Christmas. He also told Grandpa, "I love you." The mother was holding her son lovingly the whole time.

When they finished talking and the husband took the phone, she squeezed the little boy and said, "You are the sweetest son in the whole world!", as she kissed and hugged him. I said to myself, she feels the same as I do about my son. They played in the lobby while we waited to be told it was time to board the plane.

Once I was seated, I noticed a gigantic "fear" thought trying to take over my peace and ruin my entire trip back home. I thought to myself, "I will not have this." I immediately began talking loving thoughts to myself about my safety and the safety of others on the flight. I saw Christ in front of the video screen that was ten rows ahead of me. I envisioned blue light all around the plane. I invoked the power of the Reiki* symbols to empower the mechanical wiring of the plane. *(See Appendix, Natural Healing Modalities.)* I silently told everyone on the plane, "You are blessed and in Divine care." I was then stilled and filled with peace and a *knowing*. I listened and heard that because of my prayer and blessing for everyone that everyone on the plane would be blessed even though they were not aware of it.

I was told that it is only necessary for one person to bless thousands and the faith of that one person will transform all others to a place of higher consciousness. Doubts tried to persist and find a tiny little crack in my faith, but I would not allow it. A flood of warmth and peace enveloped me again and for a longer period of time.

I got up to go to the lavatory that was in the rear of the plane. There were five lavatories available, but the occupied sign was on in each one. I waited for one to become available. As I did, the mother who had the toddler whom I mentioned earlier appeared. All of a sudden she was coming in my direction. As she came closer, she started to pass me. I told her that all lavatories were occupied. She stopped and said, "Okay." Two seconds later, she looked up at me as she had been holding her head down and said, "You're not afraid to fly?" Without any hesitation, I said, "No," very calmly.

How did she know I was not afraid? Was she tied into "something" happening within me? Was peace written all over my face? Her body and her thoughts said, "Hmmm", as she folded her arms across her chest and held her head down in thought at which I had just said. She seemed to be considering the conviction with which I spoke.

My answering her question strengthened my conviction even more for the rest of the flight and I am positive that my answer hugged her and gave her strength too because that's how miracles work in the realm of time. Nothing is a coincidence. My noticing her in the lobby was not a coincidence.

The miracle is an expression of an inner awareness of Christ and the acceptance of His Atonement.(*See Glossary*) It may touch people, many people you have not even met, and produce undreamed of changes in situations, which you are not even aware of.

Evidently, while I was with this family in Christ consciousness in the airport lobby, she was aware of the Christ presence also.

During the flight back to Orlando to meet Chris, who had to take an earlier flight without me, those few simple, but truthful words rang over and over in my mind all the way to our landing, beyond and now even into this book. This experience took place over seven years ago. I am very grateful for our encounter that Spirit prepared me for and I know she is too. Miracles are like that if you are **Be-ing In** your purpose. If you are One with what you are doing and not looking to the end result or thinking about something else instead of what you are doing. Miracles are natural and loving and are occurring all the time.

How To Free Yourself From Fears

Your belief in ego gives it its power. Your belief in the Holy Spirit gives **you** the **Power**. In forgiving yourself, you set yourself free. You will find you won't and don't need to attack yourself or anyone else for that matter, any longer. You will know that you are perfect in God's sight. Ego has blinded you to your perfection. When you forgive, you call upon Christ. If you condemn, judge, verbally abuse or physically abuse yourself and others, it stems from your own vision of your weakness. If you only love, you have freed yourself from fears.

What Is Your Choice?

We are the source of life. We are life. We are God. We are the source of creation. We are the source of abundance. We are the source of Divine Substance. We are the Master of our inner world, but we can relinquish that Mastership to ego. Ego is a tiny ray of light, whereas we are in reality, the Sun. If we choose to give our power to the tiny ray, we will know only limitation. We will know only lack, lust, greed, competition, anger, blame, depression, self-pity, worry, anxiety and guilt. Why choose this limited way of living without the sunlight, without unlimitlessness and the supremacy of our being?

We must choose to be the Master of our inner world, then change in the outer world will come about easily and effortlessly. The change on the inside will match what is now on the outside. When we choose to be the Master of our vibration, then no event or circumstance will change the way we will respond.

Give thanks for the glory of God working within you now instead of declaring He is not or cannot answer your prayers. That gratitude, that thanks expands that glory through you and opens the emotions that have kept you stuck for all of your life. We become free! Peace begins to emanate from you because there are no burdens. It takes choice! All it takes is choosing again!

Attempt to become One with the vibrations of these words:

> I am Master of the vibration that comes out of me and that is the truth! No thing nor person can ever change that. If the vibration of my energy is self-pity, powerlessness, hurt, fear or anger then that is my

experience. I am the vibration and the vessel of that experience. I choose my vibration and the experience. I choose to be in harmonic resonance with God. I Am One with God.

Let us take our most precious gifts, our mind, heart and soul and consecrate them to God every morning before we get out of bed and surrender all to Him. He will not lead us astray. He WILL NOT LEAD YOU astray, but your ego will. The choice is yours! Do you want to be sick or WHOLE? Do you want to be able to say, "I love you"...to yourself?

Brief Points of Chapter

- How do error thoughts control my life?
- Six steps to "get" any disease.
- Six steps to attract wellness.
- The miracle is an expression of an inner awareness of Christ.
- How to release yourself from fear.
- Choosing to be the Master of your life.

Learning How To Be Free

Living the life I lead is fun.
Sparkling, bubbly and more.
I can soar to the clouds and the stars if I
Like or
I can play with my child on the floor.
Peeping 'round every corner,
His eyes glistening with glee
Hiding from me but not very far
Learning how to be free.

Daya Devi-Doolin

CHAPTER SEVEN

HOW TO STOP SAYING I HATE YOU... TO YOURSELF!

Did My Mind Program This?

What are we programming our minds to manifest for us? Some of us are telling ourselves things like:

I can't.....
I don't know how.....
I am stuck in this ....
I am sick, weak......
I am a victim.......
Everyone seems to be better than me....
I can't be perfect.
I am not perfect.

Or, are we doing things to punish our bodies for being the way we think we are?

Smoking (illegally or legally).
Drugging ourselves either legally or illegally.
Drinking excessively or socially.
Overeating.
Abusing children
Abusing wife, husband.
Abusing ourselves mentally/emotionally.

This is only a small sample of how we prove to ourselves that we hate ourselves and that we have the right do so. Since we think we hate ourselves and that God of course must as well, we then permit others to treat us as we believe we deserve to be treated. By our very actions, we teach others they have a reason to hate us as well.

This transfers to our relatives, neighbors, business associates, and co-workers. It transcends to nations, all in total response to how we disrespect ourselves (our response to what we think of ourselves).

Why Would I Abuse Myself?

Why do we abuse ourselves and then allow others to do the same to us? We do it to prove we are right about our "inadequacies", but say at the same time, "I wish I could change my habits of destruction, or I wish I could change my life, my world, but I don't know how." The main reason we do this is because we have made ourselves believe we are separate from our Source. We want to believe our ego is the real God/Goddess when in actuality it is only one single particle of the Source. It wants us to believe it is the Source.

It is we ourselves who have mis-created. We have created our own ego, which is our thought or illusory system. Because we created our own ego, we created the belief system that says it is the one that's right, true in all cases, at all times. Our acceptance of its existence burdens us, controls us, puts fear, guilt, blame and anger into our make-up and makes us feel powerless.

Ego Hates The Body

Although we created our ego, the ego hates the body. It cannot accept it as its home. That is why we end up punishing ourselves daily, even though we tell ourselves tomorrow it will be different...maybe or I hope so.

Ego perpetuates its control over us by causing us to be unaware of what it is doing. It makes you think God is your enemy. It keeps you doing "busyness things", non-essentials to keep your true mind, your God-Mind from being available to you because of the loud clacking sounds of "ego".

The Big Question

What For? What am I smoking for? What am I really smoking for? What am I poisoning my mind for, my body? Why am I attacking others and myself? You have to want to hear the answer and want to listen. You will get the answer.

At the base of all the various questions will be FEAR. Fear of not being loved, fear of not being forgiven, fear of oneself, fear of being old, getting old or anxious about one thing or another.

The Answer

The answer to dissolving the fear has always been waiting for you, within you. The answer is the Holy Spirit. When you have a decision to make about whether to get another cigarette for example, you will learn that ego always has an accusatory, constant, loud voice, clamoring for your attention. It will give you all the reasons you need to justify another cigarette, or another reason to steal one last time, or another reason to hurt one last time. "You should do it now, before it's too late", for example. "Too late for what?", you could ask yourself. It's the same way with overeating, or hurting someone dear to you or injuring a stranger through violence.

Ego will give you all kinds of false reasons to justify your actions. On the other hand, the Holy Spirit's Voice is very gentle, quiet, firm and loving. Whether your ego tells you that the Holy Spirit does not exist does not matter. In fact, your ego knows when you awake from the dream, it will be dissolved. So, it would never want you to be aware of your true Self anyway. That is why it keeps you involved in the non-essentials I mentioned above. We try to justify our actions.

Do Not Be Dismayed

You cannot know you are separate from God if you are involved in knowing that your "self" is God. But do not be dismayed, because through all your conflicts, God is always directing you through the Holy Spirit, through each step you take. The steps become shorter and shorter, less painful when you actually invite the Holy Spirit to accept, dissolve and erase all your error thoughts, your "fears of nothingness", as H. Emilie Cady says in **How I Used Truth**. (*See References*).

God Is Mind

The Son of God (you, Christ-mind) is the thought or the idea. The Holy Spirit, is the action or Executive Will of God. It is the part of Trinity that carries out God's Plan of Salvation within us.

The Way To Hear

The only way to hear the Holy Spirit's Voice is to invite the Holy Spirit to be your only invited guest. You have spent your life listening to the voice of ego and never knowing constant joy or happiness. Now you have the chance to begin listening to the only voice that can bring you joy. You won't have to sacrifice anything.

You have to invite the Holy Spirit every second, every minute of every day until it becomes so automatic that you are aware of the Voice for God. It will become as natural for you as breathing without thinking about it.

You can be sure that once you do this, you will only hear what is best for you in all situations, all affairs, all the time.

True Direction

The Holy Spirit does not force, coerce or control you. You have always had free will, always will have free will, but when you learn that God's Will knows far better what is best for you, then you will gladly surrender "your will" to God and know that "Thy will be done." This far surpasses what we could ever imagine to be best for ourselves.

The Reason Why You "Seem" to Have Trouble

The reason why we seem to have trouble escaping from the clutches of the fear we made is that we made fear and believe in that which we have made. We feel we would have nothing if we stopped believing in our "self". According to the Course, "Fear is the root of problems and is a call for Love."

What Will Forgiveness Do For Me?

Forgiveness is not for anyone but you. As you forgive, you will also be embracing others in your forgiveness who will then be set free. You will be released from your burden of unforgiveness. You will be given bail to get out of jail, no longer in an imprisoned state of mind.

What will forgiveness do for me?

- It will free you from the mental illusory chains that had bound you for so long.
- It will remove the sense of weakness you felt that smoking had over you.
- It will remove the sense of powerlessness you feel with food, drugs.

- It will remove the sense of aloneness you feel and the sense of weakness for making loved ones feel your brutality.
- It will remove the strain and fatigue you feel in parenting your children or relationships with family and friends.
- It will remove the guilt, anger, anguish, pain and fear you feel on the job, marriage or relationships.
- It restores your innocence.
- It restores your power and erases the need to drink, do drugs, smoke, lust, commit adultery, gamble, be jealous or be abusive.
- It restores your Oneness or connection with the Christ consciousness within you.
- It re-unifies you with the Holy Spirit. You become knowing in every sense of the word.
- It removes stress, pain and strain from all layers of your aura. (*See Glossary*)
- You could look and feel ten to twenty years younger!

There are probably about sixty million other things that forgiveness will do for you but you have to be the one to find that answer. You can start by using the spiritual journal in the back of this book to begin making your forgiveness list. You will begin to start feeling wonderful, grateful, healed and happy about life!

Give yourself permission to begin listing the people and circumstances in your life that you wish to release and to be free of. Clean out that closet that is filled with old thoughts that you cannot wear anymore, old useless feelings that you no longer need.

Rapid Healing

Forgiveness and gratitude create rapid healing over any situation but gratitude goes even further. (as explained in Leonard

Orr and Sondra Ray's book, **Rebirthing in the New Age** and as expressed in the Course.)

For example:

- Forgiveness - I forgive myself for being powerless about not smoking, eating, lusting and attacking others verbally, emotionally or physically.
- Gratitude - I am grateful for all things and to everyone and everything that has been done to help me quit smoking, quit lusting, quit attacking others, quit cheating!

How To Experience Living In The Present

Affirmations are positive statements and controlled thoughts that put you in the state of consciousness with your desires NOW. They come from the executive Will of God as thoughts to you in answer to your prayers. Use of affirmations give you control of your mind and allows God to further give you what was already yours from the beginning. The gift of everything.

With any persistent problem you appear to have, affirmations let you do just that, take control of your mind. When you do this you are giving your mind back to God. You are not trying to convince Him to alter His natural order of things, but you are raising your consciousness to the Christ consciousness within you so that you receive what has been designated for you before your asking.

Making a positive statement with FEELING, DESIRE and FAITH puts you in the realm of the NOW, as already having your desired end; therefore you have no need. There is no lack in your life. You are no longer in need of abundance, prosperity, healing, wholeness and love because you are these things already.

Do You Believe In Your Sickness?

For those of you who believe in your sickness, your weakness, your in-harmonious relationships, you can just as easily believe in your WELLNESS. Our sickness is put upon ourselves by the ego within, making us or convincing us to believe we have to punish ourselves for being "bad". We (our ego) condemn ourselves and believe we actually deserve to be sick, powerless, alone, weak or imprisoned (figuratively or literally). It is all an illusion.

Is it fun believing a lie about yourself? WE CAN REMEMBER to BELIEVE the TRUTH about ourselves by knowing we are NOT separate from God! He can only come to our awareness through our free choice, our invitation as mentioned before. If we deny His help, deny His existence within our lives, then our mental illusions about sickness of any kind are sure to continue. We then wonder (attack God) why He let this happen to us, or them, or her. We wonder, "Why, doesn't He help poor little old me?"

Ego works through attacking our Creator and us so we will not have to "straighten up and fly right." But when we realize ego's attack thoughts are only attacking our invulnerability, then ego is rendered meaningless in our lives forever.

The only way to be in control is to give your ego over to the Holy Spirit to be completely undone. To be the one in power as God created you, to know and remember that you are in control, is to give up ego without a fight or struggle. That is the way it is.

Why don't you turn to your journal pages now and write an affirmation along these lines for yourself, such as:

- I am grateful for this moment and to be able to willingly surrender all thoughts of weakness to the Holy Spirit to be dissolved and re-interpreted for me. Thank you Father! Yes!

As you say these words, feel them down deep within your heart and you will feel the Holy Spirit is quickening you. Tears may stream down your face, you may feel total bliss, you may feel the silence like you never knew before. You will be able to feel and KNOW, IT IS DONE! You may even silently hear, IT IS DONE AND SO IT IS!

Worry no more as to whether your prayer has been answered. You have released your problem into very capable hands and shall be delivered that moment from the control of ego. But you must believe it is so before it will be so. You must not try to take the steering wheel back out of the Hands of God or try to "keep your little finger on the wheel... just in case."

The Forgiveness Process

Forgive yourself for forgetting who you really are; for forgetting you are the powerful one; for forgetting you are the TRUTH, the WAY and the LIGHT. Forgive yourself for believing in the illusion that you are a smoker, an overweight person, an ugly person, a hateful person, a cruel person. These are all mis-creations of ego, not creations of God. God knows there is no ego, only as what we believe in our minds.

"Nothing real can be threatened. Nothing unreal exists. Herein lies the peace of God", according to the Course. God knows that we have never done anything to be forgiven for and He has never condemned us for any thing. In ego's mind, He has condemned us but that also is illusion.

What Is Our Salvation?

Forgiveness is our salvation from negative habits, negative relationships and negative situations in our lives that we have mis-created. Actually nothing is negative. We merely perceive through ego's eyes the things we wanted to label as good or bad in order to justify our actions for being unforgiving.

One of my clients had called for an appointment because of an inability to breathe through the nostrils. Almost immediately after our consultation had begun, her father's presence came before me and I was told he was involved in part of the cause of her physical situation. I have never met her father nor have I seen any photos of him. He was just offered last rites one week ago. He is a ninety-year old man and has suffered several strokes. He and his brother are responsible for abusing my client when she was a child but they have denied it all her life.

When she had arrived, I sensed her dad wanted to speak to her through me. I resisted it. Then I was impressed with an urgency that I must allow him permission to speak. It was a heaviness in my field of energy. I was told by Spirit it would be okay to offer my permission and so I did unsure of what was taking place. I was a bit hesitant to say the least.

Tears started to fill my eyes because I knew something profound was about to happen. I did not want my client to be hurt by whatever he wanted to say.

In a loud, booming, disgusted and angry voice he shouted, "I HATE YOU...(client's name was spoken here)!" as he yelled the name of his daughter. He continued, "You've been a thorn in my side. I hate you! You make me see myself! I don't want to be reminded how ugly I am! You are miserable and so am I. I can't stand it - I don't want you reminding me of how terrible I am, how mean I am, how ugly I am. I mistreated you (as a child). I am reminded of it every day I see you. That's why I hate you! I'm tired, tired, tired. (I made a loud clapping sound with my hands.) I want to get on with it. I want to leave you and your mother. I hate HER, too! She never did anything - slinking around all the time. It was DISGUSTING. I should have left her a long time ago. I am not sorry for what I said - if I could have, I would have left long ago. Disgusting!" (I made more clapping sounds with my hands. The clapping I am told by Spirit is breaking up that negative unforgiving energy towards my client. I sensed it as an electrifying and purifying vibration as I do it).

Once I am gone, I won't have to look at you and her any more or feel these feelings any more - disgusting! I should have gotten out a long time ago - now it's too late! What am I going to do?!"

He continues, "I could ask for your forgiveness, but I'm very stubborn - I won't ask you! I don't see that it would help, or how. I WON'T ask you! I do ask, (he uses name of daughter)! I do want you to forgive me, because I can't forgive myself for all I did to you. I didn't mean to hurt you. Jack's (name changed to protect individual's confidentiality) intention was not to hurt you, either. I allowed that - I'm sorry!

I am lost. I am truly lost! No wife and no daughter - nobody loves me - even myself. What am I to do? This goes through my mind 100 times a day. I wish I could have loved you, (daughter's named used here.), but you remind me too much of myself, and I don't love myself. I don't know what's going to happen to you! I am going to the other side soon. The best thing I can do is (words were lost here). If you can forgive me; but I don't ask that now. I'm afraid to ask you, but I will. Will you forgive me, (daughter's name)?"

His daughter responded, "Yes, I do forgive you!"

Father's response: "I believe you. Thank you. Tell me that again, looking into my eyes."

Client responded: "Yes, Dad, I forgive you - and I love you."

Father's response: "Please tell your friend, (Daya) thank you for allowing me to speak through her. I didn't know whom else to turn to. I love you (daughter's name). I wish I could have shown love." (I was clapping my hands again. I now know my clapping was severing and transmuting the negative energy thought forms that had been binding the daughter to the father by his hatred towards her.)

This has never happened to me before with a client. It was a totally new experience. Because Spirit knows I am always open to be guided by the Light, I chose to be used as a channel for her father's Higher Self. This enabled him to communicate through me and gain forgiveness from her while still on this earth's plane.

After the session, I was able to draw her father's face as I saw him appear. I was told during the session, she needed to cry and to cry soon. She had been blocking herself from feeling any emotions (sadness, anger, pain) and that was causing her to be blocked in her olfactory canal. She had been to the hospital emergency ward the night before I saw her and she tried every natural and medicinal means of alleviating the problem which had not eliminated the discomfort. I offered a Reiki session to her in addition and she was fine within a short period of time.

The Beginning Of Acknowledgment

I allowed her father's higher self to speak through me. He knew he had to clear up this bond of negative energy between he and his daughter. He cannot physically vocalize his feelings because of the strokes. He knows his time for transitioning is just about at hand. He had come to the realization of acknowledging he needed help and he had to have asked God to show him what to do. He knew he did not know how he could be forgiven by his daughter. He placed his problem in God's hands and the answer was there for him.

Perhaps we can begin to acknowledge and affirm strongly that:

- I love myself unconditionally every minute of every day!
- I am grateful I am healthy, beautiful and whole.
- I am grateful I am loved and that I love everyone.
- I am no longer destructive against myself or anyone else. I love everyone, everywhere and everything.
- I am grateful I no longer choose to be angry about anything.
- I no longer need to worry about anything. That is not my responsibility.
- There is nothing to fear. Time, age, poverty, death, loneliness no longer have any meaning in my life. They no longer rule me. God is the strength in which I trust. There is nothing else!
- I no longer need to fear myself for I am full of Love. I am Love.

What About Jealousy?

If you have found yourself in a jealous relationship and don't know why you can't handle it, ask yourself, "What am I afraid of?" Being afraid or fearful means love is missing within you, or rather you believe love is missing within you. You don't love yourself and you can't imagine why anyone else could love you. So when they do love, you try to prove this love wrong by chasing it away from you and so prove yourself "right" even though mistaken.

The real truth is that you are loved and always have been by your Creator. You have created this illusion and told yourself it is not OK to love yourself for one reason or another. You have said, "I can't love myself because my hair is too fine, too thin, too curly, too red, my lips are not the right size, my body is too fat, too small, too short, too tall or my breasts are this way or I don't think like others."

Temptations

Whenever you feel "tempted" to attack yourself or another or you just want to take one more puff or one more drink, **surround yourself with the Presence of God.** This will be in the form of powerful affirmations, **Super Vita-Mind** caplets. Say them out loud, put them on a cassette or Walkman so you can immerse yourself in the energy of the truths alone and feel the cleansing. Let them dissolve into the auric field surrounding you. Do this several times a day at the same time of the day if possible. Your cells will love looking forward to the time released, energized thought forms. They will breathe a sigh of relief.

Here are a few examples. The ones in quotes are from **ACIM:**

- "The Holy Spirit is my only invited guest. Fear and anger are not!" I relinquish anger, hatred, bitterness, resentment, jealousy and lust.
- I relinquish the need for these qualities. This means that I am in control of the forces of ego.
- I release hatred, jealousy and error thoughts into the Hands of the Holy Spirit.
- I welcome the Holy Spirit into this situation, into my life now.
- The Light of the Holy Spirit dissolves ego. "Only Truth can reside here."

- I have no reason to hate myself any longer.
- I am no longer afraid of myself. I Love Me! It is all right to love me!

Don't allow yourself to become angry for doing the things ego has had you believing it was all right to do. Do not blame yourself or condemn yourself. That is how you keep yourself in the trap you are trying to get out of by doing so.

Be grateful that the Holy Spirit is now showing you the Light about your nature and about your ego nature, which does not really exist as I have said before. Be grateful your eyes are no longer blinded to the Truth. Be grateful you have picked up this book or has it been a gift to you by someone who loves you.

Seventy Times Seven

There is a technique that has been handed down from generation to generation from biblical times that Catherine Ponder mentions in her book, **Prosperity Secrets of the Ages**. *(See References)*.

If someone did what another felt was an injustice, they were advised to forgive them seventy times seven or seventy times a day for seven days. This was Jesus' answer to Peter when Peter asked him about forgiveness. In essence what Jesus was telling him was that we should give up our hateful feelings towards that person or situation until we no longer felt any bitterness towards him.

We may need to forgive him one time or 1,000 times until it comes from our heart and we know, IT IS DONE! This applies to us as well. You can use this technique in forgiving anyone or any situation you feel may be unjust. You can also show your gratitude to the Holy Spirit yourself by writing seventy things you are grateful for, for seven days. You will see some very natural things begin to form in your life by doing both of these practices.

You could write twenty-five things you are grateful for in the morning or say them aloud or silently, twenty-five of them at noon and twenty in the evening before going to bed. Another method is to repeat the things you are grateful for as you are driving along in a car. Make a game of it with your partner or friend in whom you trust.

Perhaps you could record these things you are grateful for or are forgiving on a cassette and play it on the way to work, back home or as you jog, ride a bike or whatever you love doing. One of the lessons from the Course is, "Let me recognize that my problem is already solved."

When you are involved in any struggle, conflict or unhappiness that ego has manufactured, know these words and they shall be true:

- I no longer need to feed my ego. I am free. I am free from the chains that once bound me.

It's Ok For Me To Ask For What I Want

You have permission from God to not hate yourself. You have permission from God to forgive yourself, to love yourself, to love others and forgive them for what you perceived them to have done to you. It is OK to ask for what you want from Him. It brings Him nothing but pure joy to give you your heart's desires. Your heart's desire cannot be realized, though, until you realize that His heart's desire is Yours and you accept His gift.

> "Let us be still an instant, and forget all things we ever learned, all thoughts we had, and every preconception that we hold of what things mean and what their purpose is. Let us remember not our own ideas of what the world is for. We do not know. Let every image held of everyone be loosened from our minds and swept away."-**ACIM**

Brief Points of Chapter

- How to stop saying I hate you…to yourself!
- Why we abuse ourselves.
- The Big question.
- The Answer.
- The way to Hear.

- How to free yourself from fear.
- What forgiveness does for you.
- Rapid healing.
- The forgiveness process.
- It's OK to ask for what you want and get it.

Shooting Stars

Shooting stars.
What are they shooting?
Rays of laughter, rays of hope
Rays of wonderment on a rope.
Expectancy.
Innocence.
What are they shooting?
AWWWWWWWWH mixed with joy.

Daya Devi-Doolin

CHAPTER EIGHT

100,001 THINGS I AM GRATEFUL FOR

Why Gratitude?

I found that being grateful opens the door for more astounding blessings to overflow your cup of need and desires. Being grateful tells the universe you are truly satisfied with the gifts it has bestowed upon you thus far. Being grateful de-crystallizes all negative vibrational frequencies from your auric field, leaving you with a light filled body, mind and spirit.

Being ungrateful to life says you are dissatisfied with its gifts that have been given you and that anything more would not be welcomed. You will not receive all the good that the universe has in store for you until you are ready to change your mind about being ungrateful.

I shall share with you my 100,001 things I am grateful for so that you may take a different look at your life and see your 100,001 miracles as well.

No one had to tell me to do this. Basically, I wrote these "thank yous" for my own satisfaction. By doing so, I have benefited immensely. I am happy to now share them with you! Perhaps you can think of 100,001! Yes! It could be as much fun for you as it was for me. As a matter of fact, I hope it will be "funeasy" for you too.

The Power Behind Gratitude

It does not seem so long ago that my husband and I realized or remembered we had a Christ Consciousness. A Christ Mind. A consciousness that could decree anything, achieve anything in a Christ-like way. A Divine Way. We re-discovered our new awareness through the many books by Catherine Ponder, Charles and Mrytle Fillmore of Unity School of Christianity, Emmett Fox, Dr. Jerald Jampolsky, **ACIM** and the like.

Now I "know" I can do anything, be anywhere, visit anywhere at will; speak with my Cosmic brothers and earthly brothers at will. I now know Christ-Mind is Everything.

As a result of my knowing, I know I am One with all things and I am at peace anywhere.

While doing the Course's workbook, I came to know that I wanted the Father Mind of me to vibrate with my knowledge of how thankful I was for everything. I wanted to be specific and touch everything with my thought and my love. I wanted to magnify the glory of my Creator by showing how grateful I am. I decided to make a list of everything I was grateful for and shout it to the universe.

This chapter about my 100,001 gratitudes does not literally contain that amount. For me it merely means there are a lot of things I can focus on being grateful for to enrich my life and those around me. As you read, put your important names in place of mine.

1. I am thankful to know how the molecules of seemingly solid objects like a tomato are constantly in motion though it appears stationary and solid.
2. I am thankful to know my blood is capable of sustaining all my cells and loving all of my body.
3. I am thankful to know I am healthy, youthful, trim and beautiful. I am thankful to know Your nucleus is in everything.

4. I am thankful to know I am a Holy Child of God.
5. I am thankful I know I am pregnant and expecting a Holy Child of Love, to train in the ways of the Lord, to love and share life with his father and Dear One.
6. I am thankful that all my food is transmuted into LIGHT, ENERGY and LOVE; that it is assimilated, metabolized and eliminated easily and effortlessly; that it is God's responsibility to do so and not mine.
7. I am thankful I am Light and am being filled with love each and every second of every day.
8. I am thankful I have become unencumbered by fear, doubt, dis-satisfaction and condemnation.
9. I am thankful I meet God's manifestation in the flesh every day of my life through my husband and sons, my family members, and my planetary brothers and sisters.
10. I am thankful I love you Father and that you are the door to everything.
11. I am thankful I see the Christ Light in my brothers everywhere.
12. I am thankful I see music in the earth song. I am thankful for all varieties of music and to know it is God in action to bring us closer to Him.
13. I am thankful I help people to see they are no longer dimwitted, out of shape, dull, unintelligent, lonely, ill, sick and diseased or filled with limitation anymore. I see them as whole as I would see myself for they are a mirror of my consciousness.
14. I am thankful to be changing the race mind with other masterminds of God.
15. I am thankful for the molecules of water I drink that flush my cells with energy and light.
16. I am thankful to you Father for ending my need to be satisfied by material stimulants and needs.
17. I am thankful I am given time to read and write articles and books which prosper others and which help them to grow.

18. I am thankful I write excellent, meaningful love songs.
19. I am thankful I need only to listen to the Holy Spirit and that the Holy Spirit's Voice is what I choose to hear.
20. I am thankful I am no longer dissatisfied with the way I look or looked in the past or will look in the future.
21. I am thankful I was led to forgive myself for how I perceived myself and how I perceived others.
22. I am thankful for **ACIM** being attracted to my life and to Chris'. I am thankful I was seeking to know myself and that my Higher Self knew just where to draw help for myself.
23. I am thankful, Father, you have always seen me as perfect and whole and that you communicated that to me through the Holy Spirit.
24. I am thankful I am working my way to completion and knowing I am One with You.
25. I am thankful to Jesus for being my guide, teacher, Savior and an inspiration to me to know that I too could overcome ego and ascend to my rightful place.
26. I am thankful to Rick Maida of Massachusetts for sharing the Course not once, but twice, with us until we got the message to read it; and to Laura for Sondra Ray's book.
27. I am thankful to have a child on the way.
28. I am thankful that I now have two beautiful sons, Tyler and Joseph. They are both truly loving, have beautiful souls, beautiful eyes, minds and bodies. They are very spiritual, peaceful, happy and wise children.
29. I am thankful that I have fingernails.
30. I am thankful for the many thoughts that have helped me to grow in consciousness of Christ.
31. I am thankful for the many songs I have been able to receive from the Holy Spirit and to write them so beautifully.

32. I am very thankful for the wonderful musical partner and husband I have been blessed with. I love sharing and writing music with him.
33. I am very thankful people all over the world want to hear our songs, feel our songs and see us perform them.
34. I am thankful we are the channels now, through our consciousness, that You would have us be, and thankful to join with other people who are now helping mankind to know Your Oneness to be rid of lack, disease, poverty and unhappiness.
35. I am thankful I have learned that I am a beautiful person either alone or the presence of others.
36. I am thankful that I write beautiful, helpful books and that I am guided in each one by those of the Great White Brotherhood.
37. I am thankful that I desire to open my Faith Center by surrendering it to the Holy Spirit so that I might know true joy, truth, wisdom, strength, love and harmony.
38. I am grateful to know I no longer **need** to eat because I am sustained by Divine Satisfaction.
39. I am thankful to the universe for giving me all these wonderful books to read. For these wonderful cassettes that enhance all my mind cells to embrace other dimensions.
40. I am grateful I bring such joy love and happiness to Chris and my two boys.
41. I am thankful I am a Light Being thriving on the only substance that is necessary, Life Force.
42. I am thankful my vision has been restored, my smell, taste, my feelings, my emotions, my legs, my blood, my gums, my teeth, my hair, my skin, my organs, my nerves, my vertebrae, my brain, my toes, my feet, ankles and that they are all in the Light, constantly being bathed by cosmic rays every second.
43. I am grateful for all my beautiful clothes, all our money, my beautiful transportation, computers,

musical engagements, tours, and my awareness of divine abundance.

44. I am thankful that I am Holy and that I know I am Holy. I know I can bring out the Holiness in others by recognizing their Holiness.
45. I am thankful, Father, that Ty has a date for his prom. I am thankful she is as beautiful as he is. I am thankful she treats him as special as he deserves to be treated. I am thankful he recognizes her beauty too and that they have a safe, happy funfilled prom night to remember. (Actualized 3/25/89.)
46. I am grateful for all who call upon us for services (music, writing, speaking and healing) and who desire to pay for our loving service.
47. I am grateful, Father, your Will is being done in my life and our lives together.
48. I am thankful for my two sons Ty and Joseph, my husband Chris, Mom and Dad, my brothers and sisters Lee, Michael, Dede and Dara, nieces and nephews, aunts and uncles, my first true friends Monetta Harris, Shirley Satterfield, Mae Vershier, Gale McNiff, for Ma and Pa Doolin, all my in-laws, cousins and their children and not least, my Unity family around the globe.
49. I am thankful, Father, you have loved me through all of my illusions, struggles, my false appearances and perceptions of littleness.
50. I am so thankful Lord that my voice is filled with your substance when I sing or speak.
51. I am thankful Chris, Ty, Joseph and I work in harmony for your Good.
52. I am thankful your power is bestowed upon Chris, Ty, Joseph and others as well as me.
53. I am thankful, Father, for all the people who want to help prosper us and who do so, and who have helped prosper us and loved doing so.

54. I am thankful for all the wonderful trips you have blessed us to take and that we have gone on.
55. I am thankful we have been strongly recommended to perform at the International Unity Association of Churches Convention in Orlando.
56. I am so thankful you taught me to play the guitar so beautifully and powerfully.
57. I am happy and thankful you have provided the time, the recording studio, equipment, money and the wonderful record of songs that is in your mighty plan to have manifested shortly.
58. I am thankful I am Love.
59. I am thankful, Father, I am Light.
60. I am thankful I know I AM Christ-like.
61. I am thankful I AM Strength.
62. I am thankful I AM Abundance.
63. I am thankful I AM The Word.
64. I am thankful I AM Divine Substance.
65. I am thankful ego no longer controls my consciousness.
66. I am thankful I have power over my thinking about food, finances and all situations in my life.
67. I am thankful Father for the bones you have given me that are so pure, whole and filled with light and energy. So much flexibility.
68. I am thankful, Father, to know that the twelve apostles keep order and harmony all throughout my body, mind and spirit.
69. I am thankful for this earth school.
70. I am thankful for my never ending Life Force, for the cosmic rays that are always penetrating my Be-ing, serving me with pure energy.
71. I am so thankful Father for the unfoldment of the sacred pattern which had been trapped inside my soul and that I don't have to be re-born in death, old age or childhood rhythm again.

72. I am so very thankful for the wonders you have been preparing us to witness and experience.
73. I am thankful Lord for the many television appearances, concerts, radio interviews you have planned for us and for the many millions of people we have met and touched with our music, love and books.
74. I am thankful Father my mind thinks your thoughts.
75. I am thankful my FAITH bathes me in its splendor each and every second.
76. I am thankful, Father, there are no more unsatisfied dreams, desires or needs in my heart. I am grateful to know my desires have already been fulfilled since the beginning. I am thankful you have replaced my desires with fulfillment and satisfaction.
77. I am thankful, Father, I am the Power and the Presence.
78. I am thankful for my Breath.
79. I am thankful for the classes we teach, for the love we bring and receive from each and everyone.
80. I am thankful, Father, I surrendered the struggle to go it on my own and that I live in your WILL NOW and know such wonderful joy that I could never have brought to myself as my "'self".
81. I am thankful, Father, our house in Ayer, Massachusetts has been sold and all concerned have been blessed by the transaction.
82. I am thankful for our thriving businesses.
83. I am thankful for our children Lord, our beautiful children.
84. I am thankful that all my cells know nothing except laughter, joy and love.
85. I am thankful my hands are used to do Your Will.
86. I am thankful my vision is Your vision. I commit my whole vision to you Father. There is no hurry.
87. I am very grateful my supply in inexhaustible. I am thankful that all things are ours now. We give as freely as we freely receive. My cup is running over with

goodness and love. I trust in you, Father, as my supply and I am thankful.

88. I am thankful to know my Light is the same as in all others, no brighter or lesser.
89. I am thankful to receive large sums of money for my divine services.
90. I am thankful I have a peaceful, joyful, exciting and happy husband; one who loves me truly, dearly and completely; one who is not afraid to show me his love.
91. I am thankful Ty lives with us of his own choice.
92. I am thankful I have stopped buying into the concept of being overweight. I am thankful I have released all unwanted pounds and erroneous thoughts about the extra weight.
93. I am thankful I have a brand new mini-van that is fully air-conditioned, cassette/radio, nice upholstery, seats for sleeping or sitting and space for all our musical equipment and family outing gear.
94. I am thankful, Father, that the Holy Spirit is in every part of my being.
95. I am grateful I have two wonderful children who love me.
96. I am grateful I know how to send healing thoughts and healing techniques to others.
97. I am grateful to be alive, to be here, now.
98. I am grateful to have this beautiful home and for the one I am about to receive.
99. I am thankful I can see and I am well.
100. I am thankful I have beautiful brothers and sisters.
101. I am grateful I love my brothers and sisters.
102. I am grateful I am able to write books that reach and touch people's hearts, that inspire them as I have been in many different ways.
103. I am grateful to be able to know how to share and to speak to others with love.

104. I am grateful, Father, that Ty is growing strong in your Might and is learning about the Holy Spirit within himself.
105. I am grateful that Ty is a successful young man, and will be a loving husband and father when he decides to get married, if he decides to do so.
106. I am grateful, Father, you have blessed him as I have asked when he was an infant.
107. I am thankful to be able to hear Chris tell me every day how much he thanks me for my "YOU-ness."
108. I am thankful I do not attack myself for any reason no matter what ego says I must do to be happy.
109. I am thankful I do not attack Chris, Ty, Mom or others.
110. I am thankful I see the world not as my ego used to see it.
111. I am thankful, Father, my Holiness blesses and keeps our future children safe.
112. I am grateful the Holy Spirit is always with me. I am grateful we are all guided for our perfect good.
113. I am grateful I am no longer afraid to conceive a child.
114. I am grateful to have been childless in order to know that we are not childless except in our own mind. And that our child is already ours in the invisible plane and we have formed the right conditions for it to be here with us.
115. I am thankful to have been poor because it has taught me how to be prosperous. It has taught me how to know that life is consciousness and I receive whatever I want.
116. I am thankful Father that the words of Jesus Christ, in the Course, have cleansed my mind, my thought system and purified me in constant daily light.
117. I am thankful that the Holy Spirit is guiding me to know I no longer need food to live but that the bread (truth) and blood (life force) is what sustains me in Jesus Christ.

118. I am thankful I am seeing.
119. I am thankful I see the truth.
120. I am thankful I no longer need to fear anyone or anything.
121. I am thankful there is nothing to fear about truth.
122. I am thankful I no longer need to fear seeing.
123. I am grateful that it is natural for me to be trim and to remain at my perfect weight and health.
124. I am grateful to know that I am not invisible or unimportant in the grand scheme of things.
125. I am thankful Father that we shall be visiting and vacationing in the Bahamas, Australia, Egypt, Jamaica and other beautiful places.
126. I am grateful I feed the Holy Spirit and not the ego when I eat.
127. I no longer need to feed ego because it has been dissolved and transmuted.
128. I am grateful record companies now see a need for our special blend of music, harmonies and sound. I am thankful for the agreeable contract we have been able to establish.
129. I am grateful Father that we are exciting and creative performers who inspire others to be all that they can be through your loving guidance.
130. I am thankful for the oxygen that heals me through my breath.
131. I am grateful for Mother Earth, Brother Wind, Sunshine, fire and water. I am thankful that oxygen has such a powerful effect on me and everything on this planet.
132. Father, I am grateful that your love sustains me.
133. I am grateful you taught me how to bless my body, thoughts and my affairs, other people and animals.
134. I am thankful, Father, I forgive myself for allowing others to hurt me in the past and for what I learned by this. I have learned that no one can hurt me. It was I

who perceived of myself as having been "hurt". I see the past enveloped in a light of love.

135. I am thankful Chris doesn't lie to himself or to me and that he can see the workings of his ego, that he isn't afraid of life and that he finds it as exciting as I do.
136. I am grateful that I do not resist life.
137. I am grateful I am One with You Father.
138. I am thankful I can discern the voice of ego.
139. I am thankful for having been poor. It has taught me that I wasn't poor, only that I thought I was and so I was. It taught me how to be prosperous and to know that life is consciousness. I receive whatever I want, be it positive or negative because of my level of consciousness.
140. I am grateful to know you do not attack us and you are everything but an unloving God.
141. I am thankful to know is ego is Gone. WOW!
142. I am thankful to know I am not the body, but Christ.
143. I am thankful that I relinquished my investment in this world as I project it and that I allowed the Holy Spirit to extend the real World to me from the Alter of God.
144. I am thankful Father for the title of my book, "Have You Ever Seen a Plump Plant?" Thank you for the material that shall go into it by your Will.
145. I am thankful to know everyone is my brother who can help me anytime I need help.
146. I am thankful that all is well all the time when I remain at one with God-Mind.
147. I am thankful, Father, that I give myself permission to accept and receive all the good you offer us from a variety of sources. I am thankful I can claim my good without fearing I do not deserve anything good.
148. I am thankful that I am RADIANT!
149. I am thankful that the universe supports our being winners!
150. I am grateful I forgave my Auntsister.

151. I am grateful to be financially independent.
152. I am grateful all my stored up unexpressed feelings are no longer held in my tissues or organs anymore. All unexpressed feelings have been turned over to the Holy Spirit to be immediately re-interpreted into Truth for me now!
153. I am grateful to be able to see living things all around me and to be a part of the great excitement.
154. I am grateful I am a mother, Chris' wife and a daughter.
155. I am grateful I know how to bless, heal and to love others unconditionally.
156. I am thankful Father to know how to eat light and do so with your support and guidance.
157. I am grateful the universe loves me.
158. I am grateful Chris and I were chosen to facilitate **ACIM**.
159. I am grateful that I love the Holy Spirit's Voice above all else in all my affairs.

I am going to end my list at this point. I now want to invite you to send me just one thing you are thankful for. I would like to request 100,001 readers to do so. I will attempt to read each letter sent to me.

I believe this will uplift many minds like a chain reaction and set your faith even stronger because you know it is helping others to reach the Light within. You will be helping to raise the race consciousness to higher levels, out of the fear mode into the fourth dimension.

No matter where you work, whom you work with, whom you work for, whom you are married to or not there is good to be seen and learned from all these situations. They are our teachers in disguise. They help us to overcome, ultimately, all seemingly insurmountable problems.

The Divine Solution Is Already Before You

Don't begrudge where you are right now. Be joyous that the divine solution has presented itself to you. It is being in a thankful state of consciousness that takes you out of where you think you are. Being thankful takes you into the I AM PRESENCE vibration and lifts you up out of the hate presence frequency.

No one likes to hate no matter what they may tell you. Their Beingness is love. They came from Love. They are love and they will return to Love in their consciousness when their tolerance for pain, disease and disharmony has reached its peak.

How to stop saying I hate you...to yourself will be continued in Chapter Nine's Revelations. More ways will be discussed to magnetize **Super Vita-Minds** into your energy field. There you will find more examples and reasons to begin to say, "I Love You." to yourself, and "I am truly Magnificent!"

Brief Points of Chapter

- Why gratitude?
- List of reasons to be thankful.
- How to talk to the Universe.
- The divine solution is already before you.

Birds Don't Need Glasses

While humming along
Thanking God for my thoughts,
I saw a Great Being
Fly by up above.
"Birds don't wear glasses," it said,
Swooping by.
"Have you ever wondered or
Asked yourself why?
God makes us all perfect,
I know that's a fact.
Like a fish in the sea
There's nothing we lack.
Do chickens wear glasses
Or bees in a hive?
Do flowers need spectacles?
Do ants, or a fly?
Birds don't need glasses
And neither should you.
For He's placed all His blessings and Light
Upon you.
Now that you know
That you're perfect too,
Birds don't need glasses
And neither should you."

Daya Devi-Doolin

CHAPTER NINE

REVELATIONS

Do I Choose To Hear The Holy Spirit?

Many people hear the Voice for God within themselves and choose not to listen. As the result of not listening, they run into a stone wall built up by their ego's voice. Everyone on earth, no matter whom, has the Spirit's Voice within them. Again, not everyone is listening or accepting to follow His guidance, but sooner or later it shall be their desire and choice to do so.

They will find that their tolerance for pain, suffering, troubles and lack is far less than they thought they could handle. They will remember that there must be a better way and then they will choose God's way because His Way promises only Life, Love and Peace.

Everyone has a tolerance for pain, some less and some more than others. But nonetheless, there is that tolerance level they reach in their lives when they finally give up trying it ego's way.

When you give up your way of doing things, and start living and trusting God to know what He is doing, you begin to realize and experience Revelations from His Spirit. He will be directly speaking to you revealing secrets of The Kingdom of which you are a part.

All your questions are answered when you become totally silent within yourself. Whether you are washing dishes, driving a car, bus or feeding a baby, if you are silent or at peace during this time, you will hear and see the revelations. Yes, even feel them in the very bottom of your soul. You will be overflowing with joy at the warmth and love being unconditionally bestowed upon you.

When I am totally at one with everything, I receive His messages. I write them down so I will not forget. I usually carry paper, a notebook and pen or a cassette with me. I jot down the time, the day and year I received it.

In this chapter, I will share some of these messages with you. These are the times when I had specific time to just sit and be still, pen in hand and eyes closed. I do not usually open my eyes as I write so my writing is slanted and very tiny. Sometimes I take the messages down with my eyes open but do not tune in as well as I could with my eyes closed, as yet.

The messages that have been included in this section of the book deal with Christ's Crucifixion, the "dilemma" of abused children, death, how to rear my sons in the best possible way and how to be rid of unwanted thought patterns. All of these messages have involved choosing to be quiet and listening to Spirit's Voice for a while.

12/17/87

Dear Lord,

Would you finish teaching me about what is meant by our idea of death and life eternal. I mean, can we, as I have read, actually live in our bodies 2,000 years or longer if we so choose? I know I am one with You in timelessness but how do I answer people who want to know what I believe about death and life eternal. Do we reincarnate, as Priscilla asked me yesterday, or do we go on to the other levels of consciousness, as I explained to her?

"You Are My Blessing Daya. I am well pleased with you. You are JOY magnified! What can you not know? Until illumination reaches all mankind, they will shroud themselves in the illusion of death. Death only means you are asleep.

You can hear me clearly. Do not block your mind and believe you cannot hear me. I did say you are asleep in the body. The illusion you have made causes you to believe that this is all there is to life. You can, as you told Priscilla, live to be as old as you wish. Be it 2000 years or longer, as long as you believe in your timelessness. As long as you know you are One with Me in Timelessness, so shall it be. Not everyone believes as you do or knows what you know as Truth in your consciousness.

The body only functions as you direct it. If you direct it to believe it is dying, or aging, or ill or diseased, then it must do only as you direct it. If you witness with the power of your words that it is well, healthy, full of Divine Satisfaction, timeless, ageless without blemish, then that shall be so and that is what is real, eternal.

There are many planets like yours to which evolved life forms go to in preparation for Truth until they have become realized. Everyone must and shall at their own choosing come to the realization he is not separate from His Source."

3/13/87

Revelations from the Holy Spirit today.

"As long as you struggle with ego, yourself, you are never going to win. But as soon as you relinquish your struggle unto the Hands of the Holy Spirit to undo the negative mental mass, you will be free. The negative mental mass will no longer compete for space with your normal organs and cause disease by doing so.

They will be able to go back to their normal size and space like new organs filled with new blood. Surrender yourself to be there already."

4/8/87

In listening today, I hear:

The universe provides all the food I need daily, minute by minute. This is True!! The universe has realigned my spine whether or not I feel like it has. It is OK for me to like and love myself as I am. I am perfect. I am perfect before God. I am perfect before God and so is everyone else. I am perfect before God and I do not forget that I am perfect. I do not have to act perfect as I think perfection is, I am just perfect as I always have been but did not remember.

The universe is realigning the bacteria in my mouth to be unharmful to my tissues, gums, jawbone and teeth. It is showing me how to love my mouth totally without fear. I realize and release all fearful thoughts that my mouth is independent of my thoughts and can act on its own.

6/20/87

I heard this song in my heart on the way to work.

As He Goes Ahead To Nowhere

The worrier's in his threadbare clothing
With feet that bleed from the rocky road
He feels defeated, cheated, hopeless
But he is following the way he chose.
So he's unhappy about his life
His face wrinkled up like a prune,
And he has to look with eyes cast down
Or he'd catch a glimpse of his tomb.
Now something has entered his darkness
And shown him the hidden door
No longer will he have to scratch

And crawl along the floor
He has been released from "self" to know that
He is not lost, in a world below.

10/7/87

One day at work I was taking my fifteen-minute break that was allowed and having a cup of hot cocoa. A fear thought tried to make me feel guilty and accept that I was doing something wrong to my body for drinking it. Immediately, Spirit revealed these thoughts to me.

> "The cocoa I drink is pure. All the food I eat is pure, good and maintains my well being. The water I drink is pure and maintains my weight loss in perfect harmony. All my thoughts bear divine witness to my thinness. I invite only health, beauty, vigor and right thinking. Thank you Father!"

I hear Spirit tell me next:

> "The problem of your having no car or van is already solved."

10/31/87

We demonstrated a new car with $2,000 taken off the price right away. Our trade-in car was only worth $200 but the car dealer wrote $2,000 trade-in value on the sales slip. Revelations about my Dabney cartoon character were received 4/8/87. Sayings from **ACIM** are to be written below the cartoons and character of Dabney.

Example:

> "I am the Light of the World. I have no problem that is not solved already. I am not alone."(**ACIM**) "The universe provides all I need" was the assurance I was given at the end of what I had heard.

I started work on the Dabney and Miracles book on 8/13/88 completely forgetting I had been given this revelation. **Dabney's**

Handbook on A Course in Miracles has since been completed even though I started writing **Super Vita-Minds** first in 1988.

On 12/2/87, in the silence, while standing at the window of a company I was temping for, I was waiting for Chris to pick me up. The title for a book or article that I would be doing came to me from Spirit. I heard "Little Treats", which is now a book I call, **All I Need To Know...Is Inside.** I call it a "**pocket bite**" book. You can carry it around with you in your pocket or purse and take a spiritual bite out of it wherever you may be.

"Mind Games" or "Vitamin Mind Games" (which is what you are now reading) was changed to, **Super Vita-Minds: How to Stop Saying I Hate You...To Yourself!** This is the other book I was told that I would be writing.

Then I felt these affirmations come forth from me:

My Lord loves me.
My Lord is loving me.
My lord has always loved me.
I love my Lord.
I am wonderful.
I am special.
I am not forgotten.
I am not lost, forsaken or forlorn!

12/7/87

Revelations for today:

My word quickens the life in my twelve centers. My word expands these centers and they work on universal levels. This is the second coming of Christ (subconscious awakening). The First coming is the receiving of the TRUTH into my conscious mind. I have faith in things invisible.

The universe wishes to give me everything I desire because it is God's desire that I will to fulfill and recognize. The universe has always been preparing the way for me to full vision. My thoughts have drawn unto me poor eyesight because I believed in poor vision. My spirit has known otherwise. The universe has waited and wanted to give me all the power I needed to know that I can see Now. All I had to do was to accept my true vision. I am truly grateful!

12/13/87

Father,
What can I do to let Ty know I love him?

"My Child,
You can give Tyler more of your time by being with him and not always doing things when he is with you. Talk with him. Not at him. Forgive him for being with his father and being like his father."

12/15/87

Father,
I just want to hear your words of TRUTH, your BREAD and your WATER of life to me. Thank you.

"May God's blessings and power continue to fortify you and your loved ones. Peace is yours through your understanding of the word of God. You glorify God our Father through your words of truth. You have been empowered with the gift of oneness and salvation. Your love of God has blessed you and your fellowman. You can no longer hate or see hatred.
You only see good in everyone whom you know as your brother, a divine being.
You bring peace with you wherever you go because you are peace. You are One with Peace. The money is already yours today in mind. You are to use it and bless it and vivify the word of God in all you do and I will guide you.
Chris will now know what the Law of Oneness means as you have asked me to show him so he too can know

constant joy. You have selected a special man. He will do great things in his lifetime. He will bring great love and joy to you and your children. He will teach them the meaning of love, by being love himself. He will make you very proud. He will even remember to close the closet doors for you.

I am working with you in the ethers to re-gain your memory of your physical sight. You must not falter. You are so close to seeing. Your desire is my desire and so it shall be, shortly in your mother's day. She will see and become born anew as she witnesses your transformation. I ordained that your boss give this time to you to be in the quiet where no one can disturb you or see you. Praise God. This is what I want you to do. You bring Joy to me.

Release all fear thoughts regarding food and weight by saying, "I am one with divine satisfaction." Repeat it silently and aloud when you can for 20-100x a day or until you no longer need to do so.

Be one with your breath and breathing. Your breath is where you get your substance from, not food. You don't really need food. Your body and your baby will be healthy regardless.

You were right when you affirmed you are one with vision so continue doing so for 50 x a day as you breathe. With each breath, all the chakras will be re-arranging the molecules and atoms in your eye sockets, optical nerves, arteries, muscles cells and tissues as you commanded them to do last week upon reading Charles Fillmore.

Everything you ask for you have the power to receive with no effort accept to use your faith, and believe in your oneness with the Father.

I will be revealing to you more and more of your powers the more you release all you asked to be released of.

You are a good student and always have been. Don't put yourself down for not having learned sooner. Age is immaterial as you well know. Forgive yourself or that thought pattern and be free.
I will let you know when it's time to receive more instructions. You will hear and I will answer.
Your Comforter."

12/14/87

Dear Father,
Please tell me the thought I must hold to that will free me from believing I cannot see clearly without my glasses. Which thought could I hold to help me know I see?

"You Must Know That You Can See, You Are Seeing. You Are Vision Itself, You Live And Breathe Vision."

12/15/87: 4:35 P.M. at work

Father,
What is meant by Death? I see people "die", see their bodies in caskets. Is this the right terminology? I know our spirits live eternally but do all our bodies go through the same process even though we may believe our bodies can live on forever, as for a 2,000-year period?

"My Child,
Everyone has their own belief until they know the TRUTH. You know the TRUTH. You know that you can Will whatever you desire into manifestation. People feel that I am a God of Wrath and that I, being All Powerful, use my Power to my advantage and to control humankind. They have a long road to travel but they will learn the TRUTH about themselves at their rate and level of consciousness.
Anyone can live to be as old as they choose. I do not interfere in the Laws of Cause and Effect. If I did, then your will would not be your will at all. You are free to

choose to listen to MY Will or yours but eventually all will choose to listen.

When people "die", leave their bodies behind on this earthly plane, they have chosen to do so by the thoughts they held in their minds. Some have even decided which way they shall die by the fear thoughts they embrace about life."

Why Do Children Die?

"You want to know why I allow children to die. Why don't I help them and protect them. All children are my sheep. No one is lost, forgotten or put aside.

I cannot interfere with man's will that does the harm to children. I have placed with man the Holy Comforter to lead and guide man to the Truth of his Oneness, but I cannot make him change his mind. If he chooses to harm, kill himself or others, he is given a choice to make. If he chooses fear, then the result or effect of that fear will have the form of fear, death. If man believes he is being attacked, he will attack because he feels separate from Me.

Children are innocent, pure Love, My Love. All my children have much to learn about forgiveness. They have to cross the bridge of forgiveness to Know Me, to realize this world, the world of illusion and ego is not what they want. For your soul to grow, you choose the necessary environment that you know you will learn from. Your soul gravitates to that environment like a magnet.

Your life on earth may be one minute, one day, one month, or one year but that is all you need in your experience. Your life in the presence of a couple, teaches them about forgiveness, about Love in ways you cannot see unless you desire to see beyond this world and what it offers.

Parents of children who appear to die so young, for no apparent reason, are all learning about forgiveness at their rate of understanding. All those related in a family have a common bond between them which is to seek the TRUTH, to learn what they need to learn.
Some people blame Me for their troubles but that is only for a short time. They learn that their thoughts are the cause and effect of their well being. They learn to release fear, hatred and blame towards Me and replace it with love. NO ONE IS LOST, THOUGH IT MIGHT SEEM so in the world that is seen as real."

12/26/87

Father,
I wait and listen silently. Thank you!

"My Holy Child,
You have done well today. You must continue to listen to only My Voice, in that you shall be strong and know your strength. Believe only In My sound and the joy it brings you. You will have work tomorrow. Sometimes you feel alone but I am never not with you. I know it's hard for you to believe what appears to be real but all is well. I want you to write ALL IS WELL NOW as long as you have to, until you believe it."

Heavenly Father,
Would you reveal to Tyler (my son for reader's sake) what would you have him do to succeed better in school?

"My Holy Child,
You must always be at Peace within yourself first. Then you can hear My Voice. The answers are within you. In time of doubt you are choosing not to listen to me. To be free you shall always know what is TRUTH. Be not afraid that you cannot know Me. You

are One with Me. You are Me and I you. All fears are useless."

12/26/87

Father,

Please reveal to me what I should teach Ty today and how. Thank you Lord.

"My Daughter,

I bless you for your desire to hear My Voice and listen. Show Ty the way to Peace by giving him your Peace. Say, I AM ONE with God in Peace. Go over the cards you made for him. Take him where he wants to go without putting limits on it. Offer him your heart, which is MINE. This you shall share today."

Please continue to speak to me Father.

"My Child,

You are a blessing to all those whom you meet and see. They love to be near you and touch you. Chris tells you I am well pleased with you and I AM. You must continue to believe as there is no turning back. The way will be provided for you to know. Do not be anxious because of anyone else. Do not feel guilty as ego would have you feel."

3/8/88

I hear from Spirit.

"It's all right to ask for what you want and get it!"

3/8/88 (4:00 PM)

This is what I hear today.

I AM THE BREATH OF LIFE. I AM BREATH. I AM SUPPLY.

3/8/88 At 4:20 PM, I hear:

> I need not work to earn money anymore. I am Divine Substance. I am Abundance. I am still and know that I am God. I have Supply. I have God-ness. I have Vision. I am Energy. I am Light. I am Healing. I am Music.

"My Crucifixion"

On 3/29/88 (Tuesday before Easter at 5 AM), the Holy Spirit's Voice tells me to write something down regarding the Course. It was also the day after my husband Chris and I had facilitated a study group. I said, "Thank you for choosing me as a vessel Lord."

> "There is much to be said regarding My crucifixion. There was no pain. Pain only exists when you think what you are is a body. I did not suffer. You only suffer when you believe you are separate from Our Father. When you believe there is God and then there is you. When you remember, 'I and the Father are One', there can be no pain, no suffering, no limitations. You are His Love. You are His Oneness. I and the Father are One. Sickness is the result of anger at thyself, brought on by your thoughts of guilt. Suffering and pain is the effect of the same cause, anger and guilt placed upon yourselves as you pretend to be God meting out your own punishment. You feel you must condemn yourself for your unforgiving nature as you see it. I could never be harmed or attacked because I know there is only Love. I transcended ego, so therefore I was invulnerable to harm, pain, attack or suffering.
>
> You only suffer because you "believe" you have done something wrong that is unforgivable in your eyes. You pretend it is God who is punishing you so you

make Him out to be an angry vengeful God, in order that you will not be accountable to yourself as the cause of your suffering, conflict or pain.

In order for you to know that you, too, can be resurrected from the dead, the dead way of thinking, I had to show you that you must crucify those old ways of thinking; thoughts of lack, attack, limitation, disease and pain in order to rise again through me the Christ. You cannot know God except you come through the Christ consciousness which is what I meant by I AM THE TRUTH, THE WAY AND THE LIGHT.

You must enter the KINGDOM OF HEAVEN through opening your Christ center. You do this by knowing you too are Christ, the son of the living God. By knowing you are Christ, you are one with miracles or the natural order of the universe, love. So in that realm of Christ-ness, you can do all things because you will remember that nothing is impossible.

You will be able to rearrange your molecules, atoms at will or heal anyone (of any problem or sickness) just with a thought, because you will know you are One with the Father. You will know, 'I AM JEHOVAH. I AM ALL THINGS FOR ALL THINGS ARE IN ME AND ABIDE IN ME' Amen." This section is from, **Dabney's Handbook On A Course in Miracles** (*See References*).

I was told after I wrote this revelation down that I should call my minister and ask if it could be read at our Easter Service. This I did. She received it in her heart that it should be read to our congregation on Easter Sunday and so it was. It was an extremely moving experience.

Revelation On Release

"I release myself from the teacher that work has been for me. I bless all my work and jobs for the teachers they have been to me. I release burdensome work. I let it go in heaven as on earth (my conscious mind) in love, into the hands of the universe and I accept my divine substance; God-supplies forever, starting this instant."

"I release my consciousness unto God's supply. I release myself from this job instantly now." On March 25, 1988, I was informed that my contract for the job I had just released myself from would be over on March 28th, a Monday. This came after I thanked God for the experience during my lunch break. I had been sitting on a grassy mound in meditation, prayer and in releasing. When I felt the release with all my heart, a tear fell gently and lovingly down my cheek and I knew IT WAS DONE.

"Bring Your Awareness To Me"

A friend of mine at work was having difficulty. I was given these helpful words from Spirit to share with her.

> "You are another being, one whom you have forgotten. You know only of this being when you are quiet. Your ego scares you but it cannot win in anything. You are to grasp and follow these teachings."

- Bring your awareness to Me in all humility everyday.
- Stand at your door and watch for the cries of ego as you stretch your consciousness far beyond it.
- Listen to My Voice and be made strong.
- Give me your deceptions and I will re-interpret them for you.
- Eat only when you hear to do so. Eat Light and bless your food with Light and Energy.

- Be of good Faith. I AM WITH YOU. YOU ARE MY BELOVED CHILD.

You Too Could Be One Of The Happiest People In The World

My husband, Chris, has said to me many, many times, "You are the happiest person I have ever known." We make a joke about how unaffected I am about anything. I could lose my job and still be happy. People always want to know if I am always this happy? My husband tells them, "Yes."

There is a reason for my happiness and people always want to know how I do it. How do I stay so calm, happy and peaceful all the time!?

I have many secrets. You are finding them out by reading this book. I have a little bottle full of **Super Vita-Minds** caplets which I take every day. My prescription is always filled by the Creator so I never run out. I never forget to take my prescribed dosages. I take them with me everywhere I go in my consciousness. I offer to share my dosages with you now with no ill side effects.

When I arise in the morning, I say, "Thank you Father!" It covers everything that I have encountered during the night and all I will encounter during the day. I open myself up to the miracles that wish to unfold for me and my family. Before I leave my bed, I sit on the edge and say "I surrender all my past thoughts, present thoughts and future thoughts into your hands, Lord, through the Holy Spirit." If I have nothing to concern me, then all I have to be concerned with is being happy.

I do not allow anything to worry me. I place my concerns with Christ and I trust. I am assured always that ALL is WELL. Having read **The Greatest Secret in the World**, by Og Mandino, I trained myself to let problems just drop away like water runs down a duck's back. That book shows the reader how to focus on what is important and to move forward around any stumbling blocks.

Another technique I use is to write a letter to the Creator. Here is an example:

Dear Heavenly Father,
I am ready to accept your Will in all that I undertake today. I will accept Your will in eating, living, working, loving, teaching and being. I say Yes to all you offer us without doubt and I thank you for loving me and for the family I have been given. Thank you for teaching me Thy Perfect Law and Ways. Thank you for hearing me. I know you always hear me.
Love,
Daya

When you know you are doing everything you can to be loving to yourself, you cannot be unhappy.

6/8/88

My realization on driving home to pick up Chris was that:

- There is no place that love does not exist in my body.
- There is no love lacking in my bones, cells, tissues, brain, hair, organs, limbs, face, heart, eyes, fingers.

I repeated these ideas that the Holy Spirit gave me with such joy. It lasted about 15-20 minutes before Chris came out from work.

Another secret is that I trust that my prayers are answered already and I do not try to do God's job. My job is to believe and have faith.

6/9/88

I invite the Holy Spirit to provide the right sale of their trailer for our potential buyers so they can purchase our home, if that is God's Will. We wish to purchase a house in Florida (we were renting it at the time.)

We drove up to Ayer, MA on vacation and went to pray with the prospective buyers while visiting my in-laws up there. The buyers bought our home in Ayer, MA within 3-4 months after this prayer.

> I invite the Holy Spirit to disburse our monies to our creditors and to provide the means to do so. I thank the Holy Spirit for us. I am truly grateful.
>
> I invite the Holy Spirit in the essence of Christ to heal the skin on my forearm completely, totally with no fear on my part, only love.

Inviting the Holy Spirit to be a conscious part of your daily life will certainly transform you. You will change. It will be for the better but not necessarily like you thought it would be. A serious housecleaning of debilitating thought patterns will definitely take place, if you choose to allow it, which I hope you do. The Voice is there for you to hear, soft loving and strong. Take time to sit and merge with it. You will be blessed.

Erasing Error Thoughts (Denial)

Through the revelations that I have been given over the years, thoughts of denial to the illusion that faced me helped to clear away debris from my thought system. Some of my denials are given below to help show you how you can aspire to move upwards. Denials are used to offset in your subconscious mind the illusions you hold onto as truth for your being. These are the energized thought forms that erase error thoughts from your mind through the blessing of the Holy Spirit.
The revelations that were given to me are below:

Old thought form:

- I need my glasses to see.

Denial:

- I no longer need glasses to see.
- I am ready to release the fear that I cannot see and that I cannot see without glasses.
- My eyesight is no longer defective. Right now a stronger life force has been awakened in me. My eyes are sustained by the love of God, the breath of God.

I have been wearing glasses since I was two years old and have accepted it to be the way "it is". But ever since my 21st year of life, I have been hearing, "I can see" from the still quiet Voice and that it shall be a reality. I hear I won't need glasses. I received more thought forms to embrace in the form of gratitudes.

- I am grateful all my illusions have been corrected!
- I am grateful my perceptions about my state of health have been re-directed by the Holy Spirit!
- I am grateful all my error thoughts have been erased!

The "I can't see without glasses" consciousness promotes the universe to show me how to prove this to myself according to the faith in my belief. This consciousness draws unto me all that the universe has to give to affirm this in my life, so the Holy Spirit revealed this to me:

- Cosmic rays from the universe contain all the healing energy I need to sustain and heal my vision and my thoughts about seeing.
- I am one with complete vision and sight.
- I am one with total trust in the universe and God.
- I am sight.
- I am accepting and receiving healing.
- Actually, I have already received. My awareness did not believe or accept it before now.

- I am receiving and have received total reversal of mind and thought about my eyes.
- I am claiming my eyes have forgiven all negative thoughts and have now released all negative thoughts that they have lived with and believed all these years.
- I forgive my mom and dad for any fear thoughts that I thought I might have received from them before my birth, during my birth, or after my birth.

Being one of the happiest people in the world is fun and enjoyable. It's also a lot easier than most other things that you do when you don't put your mind to it. Just let it flow like tying your shoelaces or driving. It comes from loving yourself and trusting the source of all you are.

Why not get a small bottle and label it **Super Vita-Minds**, Dr. Omnipresent as the physician, to be taken 4 x a day. Put your name and date on it. Check how you feel in one week's time and record it in your journal pages at the back of this book. Give yourself permission to have fun on your journey. We will talk about intention in the next chapter.

Brief Points of Chapter

- Do I choose to hear the Holy Spirit and listen?
- Why do children die?
- "My crucifixion."
- Revelation on release.
- Bring your awareness to Me.
- You too can be one of the happiest people in the world.
- Deny the illusions. Do not invest your power in the illusion.

"Daya, through you it shall occur. Watching your work, watching you do the Will of God, this will take you further than you can imagine. You must continue to be open to the Will of the Lord, to His Word and more and more doors will be opened to you. Ask and it shall be done unto you. We are here at your beckoned call. Your child (to be) is a Holy child, protected by the Light and given to you by the Light.....I leave you now in the Name of the Lord Jesus Christ."

Ezekiel." Channeled to Daya Devi-Doolin 2/20/94

CHAPTER TEN

INTENTION

Are There Neutral Thoughts?

Everything in life on this planet is very simple. There are basic keys given us to know this. When we forget or choose to ignore them, we suffer needlessly.

One of the very basic keys is that thoughts are things. Thoughts are energy. They travel through timelessness into unlimited boundaries. They are what our belief and intent is composed of. They bring about our experiences that are the exact and immediate results of our thoughts. Nothing is accomplished, created or invented on this earth without the thought first. Napoleon Hill once said, "All that you can conceive, you can achieve."

His son was born with no ears, but he was determined that his son would be able to hear. He was determined that he would find a way to make this happen. It did happen through his love, intent and belief.

Example: Thought = action = experience
or
Belief = action = result
or
Intent = action = result

There is no thought we can have that does not have a result or manifestation of that thought. Our belief behind the thought has given it power to manifest whatever it is that we believe. Our subconscious is our genie in manifesting anything that we want, need or believe, be it right or wrong. It is not a judge of what is right or wrong, it merely acts on our behalf and brings to us like a magnet all that we have placed into its hands to do.

Life is not about arguing who is right or wrong. You can be right all the time but miserable because of your "rightness". It is not important that you be right, but it is important that you be HAPPY!

Another very important and basic key is that no thought can come into our mind and occupy our attention except that we have chosen to entertain its presence. Everything is choice. If we want to believe something and believe it is right, no one can change our minds about it except we ourselves.

No one can put a thought in our mind that we are sick, or that we deserve to be sick except we ourselves. No one can put a thought in our minds that we are poor, our vision is bad, our body is ugly except we ourselves.

Another basic key is that we have to take charge of our thoughts at all times for there are no neutral thoughts. This means there is no thought we could ever have that would not bring about its causal result. This is an immutable universal law. If we have a thought that we realize could do us harm then we do have the power to say, "CANCEL, CANCEL", and it will be cancelled throughout the universe with no negative effect whatsoever upon us.

Another basic key to living a life full of simplicity is that of being grateful for everything that life gives us which it does according to our thoughts. It decrystallizes all the negative energy we might have stored up in our bodies. The energy might have been stored as arthritis, tumors, cancer, AIDS, gallstones, high blood pressure or diabetes as the result of our crystallized fears. Living a life that is simple, filled with love and happiness and not filled with stress, strife, fear, hatred or anxiety will bring you many blessings that have been hidden from your awareness.

The way to live that simple life is to use the Key of Love, Unconditional love, not conditional love. What is unconditional love? It is love that requires nothing of another. It does not judge another as stupid. It does not judge another as threatening. It does not judge another as incompetent. It does not judge. It does not draw energy from another for its own purposes. It does draw its energy from whatever name you choose to call it, Universal Source, Prime Creator, God, Goddess or Supreme Being.

Unconditional love towards everyone and everything will bring you the magical results that you are seeking. The intent behind your unconditional love creates the action you must take that will bring about the good you deserve.

Everyone gets back love only when they send out and radiate total unconditional love to themselves and others. There will be no mistake as to what type of love comes back to them because their intent is not to harm or take energy from another for promoting themselves higher than another.

What is Unconditional love? It's total, and complete forgiveness of ourselves and others. It is knowing there is no need for forgiveness in the first place because we merely saw the situation through conditional love eyes and we were mistaken about what actually happened. It is not *needing* to be loved because you know you are Love and you are complete. It is not demanding. It is patience.

Unconditional love allows everyone the right to make the decisions that are best for them. And it approves of their choice because it knows all decisions are based on the information we have at the time of making the choice. It knows that there are no neutral thoughts and that thoughts are things.

It knows that thoughts are energy and have form. It knows that whatever we wish to create in our lives shall be done because of our intent (belief) behind the thought. Unconditional love allows our loved ones the opportunity to experience the consequence of their choices whether It feels that it would be right or wrong for them or not good for them to experience the consequences.

What is conditional love? It is a conditional love that only loves when someone does something for you to "deserve" your love. Conditional love gives its power over to some other object or another person and resents it later on. This strong energy towards that person or condition takes lodging somewhere within the body and multiplies.

Don't Lose Your Power

You lose your power by consenting to choose to give your power over to that person or thing. You then become angry at something outside of yourself so you won't blame yourself. But in essence you really become angry at yourself for losing control.

Conditional love only loves when the daughter does what you want her to. Conditional love only loves when the son does everything you want him to do. Conditional love criticizes those who do not do what you want them to or who do not do things the way you think they should be done. Conditional love hates, discourages, breaks down self-esteem and takes energy from another to make them weak and not believe in themselves any longer. Conditional love intimidates, and interrogates. Conditional love sees everyone as wrong and unlovable. Conditional love tries to embarrass others in front of others.

Empty Handed Is Not What You Want

People who engage in conditional love do not realize that all the negative energy that they put out towards another under the guise of unconditional love comes back to them leaving them empty handed of the love they feel they deserve. They only get back the conditional love conditions they send out because thoughts are things and they manifest all that they send out. The same energy they send out is what they receive and they can't understand why they are unhappy and why they can't seem to find love.

Remember we have the power to control what thoughts we accept as ours. I always say to unwanted thoughts, "The Holy Spirit is my only invited guest", **(ACIM)** and I also know and remember that my human creations have no power over me no matter how real I try to make them. Your thoughts have power. They are the spoken Word and that Word is our gift from God.

The faith and energy we put behind our every intention gives the goals the power to manifest boldly and securely in our lives. What is more difficult to manifest in our lives? Nothing, if we but believe that it is possible. It was my intention to sit in the seat of receptivity of my highest good which entailed, a child with Chris, a better place to live, debts paid off, a metaphysical center and church, a computer to do the necessary books, articles and newsletters. Believe that you too can make your life a blessing for all whom you come in contact with as well. In the next few pages of this chapter, I am hopeful you will be inspired by the action and power behind your intention.

Why Florida?

Chris and I moved to Deltona, Florida in 1986 after living up north all our lives. He was raised in West Newton, Massachusetts. and I in Philadelphia, Pennsylvania. People have asked us why or what brought us down here. Listening to the Holy Spirit, which is the subject of another book, drew us here.

Basically, we had purchased a washer and dryer that would not be hooked up for use before we had to do another load of laundry at our friendly nearby Laundromat.

I always enjoyed looking at the bulletin board at the laundromat whenever we were there (Ayer, Massachusetts). This last visit had a diagram of a cute house on pink, neon paper that stood out. I found out it was a house in Deltona, Florida. I took the drawing down that had the phone number on it and showed it to Chris.

I heard to call the lady about it, so I did. I shared the information with Chris again. No real interest on his part. Several weeks later, I heard to call her again and asked if she had any pictures of the house that she wanted to sell. She herself lived nearby in Massachusetts. She mailed us a picture and it was soooo cute! It turned out that my cousins, who lived in Daytona Beach, Florida had decided to have a family reunion in that city. I didn't know them very well. My mother wanted to go and so we all decided to go down to Florida. It was my first trip ever to the south.

While in Florida for the reunion that was held in Daytona Beach, we decided to drive to Deltona and find the house that was on the bulletin board in Massachusetts. We went to the realtor who had the key to the house and went on a tour of the house. My mother, Chris and my older Son Tyler went to see it with me. It was wonderful. I fell in love with it. Chris was uncertain.

When we got back to Massachusetts, we arranged to rent the house from the owner until we could save up enough money to purchase it. We lived in that home on Phonetia Drive for seven years. Every time we tried to purchase it something would happen that would block us from doing so.

I am now thankful because we did not know what our Highest good had in store for us. We are just glad it worked out that way.

Miscarriage

I had experienced an earlier miscarriage in Massachusetts and another later in Florida. After we moved to Florida, we decided we would apply for adoption. We went to a couple of agencies and listened to their procedures and decided to sign up with one. We hadn't heard from them and so we put it out of our minds. A couple of years later, I became pregnant and again another miscarriage.

I began having difficulty urinating. I saw a gynecologist and was informed I had a fibroid tumor that could not be removed but that I needed to have a hysterectomy. I saw two other gynecologists and they both said the same thing. I had emergency trips to the hospital to be catheterized.

I had to wear a catheter bag outside strapped to my leg. I could not wear slim pants anymore. I had to wear baggy pants and long skirts to hide the bag. As I would walk down the aisles on my job I was very self conscious about the urine sloshing and swooshing around in the Foley bag strapped to my inner leg.

I called other people who had received hysterectomies (some patients of the doctors) to help me make a decision. I could not in good conscious go through with a hysterectomy, not when I knew we still wanted to have children. I finally had Chris take the catheter out of my bladder. I could not go through the rest of my life tied to fear.

One morning soon after that when I knew I had to make a decision as to have surgery, I awakened at 7:00 AM. I sat on the edge of our bed and told God I knew there had to be a better way and I open myself to it. I immediately went to my file cabinet and got out an ad I had saved over a year ago because I had heard to do so at that time.

How Listening Saved Me

In the previous year of my illness, I had seen an advertisement in a holistic magazine. The ad had information about a spiritual healer named Rev. Barbara Walter who lives in Largo, Florida. I saved it in my files because I had heard to do so. I knew just where to go to find it. I called her at 7:15 AM that morning as mentioned above. She could have been in Japan or somewhere else in the country travelling because she is in such demand. But she was there, waiting for my call.

She could sense the urgency and knew exactly where my trouble was. She asked me if I could get there by early morning. I told her I could. When I hung up the phone, Chris and I got ready and drove two and a half hours to get there.

She is a beautiful soul. When we arrived, she led us into a room for healing and had me lie down on a carpet. She sat about three feet away seated against a wall in front of my head. Chris was sitting alongside my thighs.

Barbara directed light energy through my entire physical, emotional and mental bodies. Colors were swirling around her and me. Archangel Michael was standing behind her as she worked. I saw several black bubbles leave my body and I knew instantly that the tumor was removed. I said, "I can see the tumor leaving me." She saw what was happening as well. She asked Chris to put his hand on my abdomen and pubic area and tell her what he felt. Chris told us that my abdomen felt very warm. He said my abdomen was no longer hard like it used to be. It was now soft. It felt different. Chris saw the colors swirling around Barbara as well. I felt wonderful.

She said I should go back to the doctor and see what he tells me upon examination. She also told me I needed to eat more carrots and cabbage. That was the message that was given her to give to me.

Reiki Enters My Life

I have a dear friend named Mary who now lives in Arizona. At the time I was going through this illness, she had just become a Reiki Practitioner. She had just become a practitioner a few days before I went to see Barbara. Mary offered to help me stabilize my condition and continue to help me mend quickly by offering Reiki. *(See Appendix)*

She would get the practice she needed by helping me and I would get better quicker, totally. After my first hour treatment with her, I knew that I wanted to become a Reiki Practitioner also so I could continue to heal myself. She introduced me to her Reiki Master Teacher, Donna Snow Spears, at a Christmas party that she and her husband gave. I could tell she was filled with unconditional love the minute we met. She is a beautiful person and teacher. Meeting her definitely changed my life. She enhanced my life. Meeting my other Third Degree Reiki Master Teachers, Rev. Dr. Constance Johnson and Lisa Lloyd has been just as mystical and empowering for me.

I went back to one of the doctors I had seen. He told me there were no tumors in my body, anywhere. After I had been into Reiki for about a year, Chris and I had begun offering holistic classes on natural healing in our home. One of the facilitators at that time is a dear friend of ours, Thomas “Sacred Bear” Young. Thomas is a

Reiki Master, Certified Clinical Hynotherapist and an Ordained Minister. He offered to do some healing with me after the workshop was over. During the healing, he noticed there was a baby boy soul in my etheric space.

Lost Baby Soul

The baby boy did not know he was not supposed to be there. He wanted to be with me and did not know where to go. Tom guided me to release him into the Light and he did the rest. It was such a magnificent experience and so reassuring. I sobbed and wept and sobbed. I had been feeling and sensing this little light being around me for years, sensing that he wanted to come into our world and live with us. This episode of my life took place in February, 1993.

In The Seat Of Receptivity

It was December 12, 1993. I had just finished reading one of our many metaphysical books that we have available, **Bringers of the Dawn**, by Barbara Marciniak. I sat in meditation and repeated the words below with feeling. A knowing came about my entire physical and spiritual body. A completeness filled my heart which is difficult to describe.

The words that I meditated on were, "I am intending the receptivity of our baby. I am in receptivity of clients who desire to be well and who are willing pay for my time and services. I am in receptivity of a new home with fulfillment of all our needs for healing and recording. I am in receptivity of recording contracts and publishers for our music and books. I am in receptivity of agelessness and timelessness with my son and husband. I command the pillar of Light to be absorbed into every DNA molecule of my body."

I made these words my intention everyday to operate in a pillar of light. I felt the light frequency connect me and fill me with protection and information. I felt it move into the base of my spine down and up my body. I felt the earth energy as well coming out of my solar plexus area like a fountain and forming a golden shield of light around me.

We were also in the receptivity energy to get out of debt shortly. From the **Bringers of the Dawn**, I used this phrase over and over, "To my Creator, and guides and all those of the Light who are assisting me in my evolutionary journey on Earth, It is my intention that I be successful. It is my intention that I am always safe in all things that I do. It is my intention that I receive love and give love in all things I do. It is my intention that I have a good time and I am provided for with prosperity according to my needs. It is my intention that I not become merely enamored of the material world. It is my intention to always be beautiful inwardly and outwardly."

I forgot about "How is it possible?", and concentrated on listening to what are the next steps I needed to take to move on. I knew forgetting about the how removes all the doubts and holes in my faith.

I Intend

Trust your feelings no matter what they are. When you are not afraid of feeling and you move past judgement and allow yourself to feel all five ways, you begin to feel. You will have a tremendous breakthrough because you will be able to ride feeling into other realities. Do not be afraid of your feelings. It is time to stop tiptoeing around things, and avoiding your emotions. Dive right into your emotions. Fear and anger can be used as a technique to move you beyond your personal boundaries. If you do not have permission to feel your anger or fear, you cannot learn. Feeling connects you with life. Just say, '"What the heck, I will go there. I surrender" Then deal with being there and don't worry about being centered.

Learn to love your emotions. As long as you describe something as difficult you are making it difficult. No one else is doing that for you. You are resisting and judging the change. You must become friends with your emotions because through feeling, you can climb the ladder to the multidimensional self, the twelve chakra system and explore you true self. (*See Glossary*)

From here on, I shall share parts of my journaling as it relates to my intentions and the magnitude of manifesting my intentions. By my sharing my intentions perhaps you will see how our intentions bring about the desired results we truly want in our lives. A change in the perception of who we think we are will allow us to begin to love ourselves in an unconditional way for the first time. We will be able to see the miracles that have been cloaked by our blindness.

December 30, 1993

Frustrated about Chris and I not being able to give birth to a child.

December 31, 1993

Joseph Paul Doolin conceived...more on this later in chapter.

January 22, 1994

Been working hard all day to get my book out, "All I Need To Know...Is Inside", and received some very strong promptings and urging to sit down, be quiet and listen. I wrote, "I am here, listening and ready to write what the Holy Spirit wishes."

"Thank you My Child for listening and settling down. You will be well rewarded. Blessings I bring you from the Pleidian Council. All doors have been opened for you. You have made it through the grid work necessary to be a multi-dimensional being. We are happy to work with you. Believe that you will find all necessary information for your next task. The Center activity is going very well, as you know, effortless and easily. You are not worrying about anything. Thank you for allowing us to work for you. Your blueprint is as follows:

- Stay in control of your thoughts, feelings and emotions.
- Believe in who you are and your impact on people. Grasp the meaning of the moment.

- Believe all the love in your heart and more will pour in. Beckon no one, they will all come to you.
- Share your truth with them...they are seeking your words and wisdom of the Law of Life.
- YOUR CHILD IS COMING! DO NOT FAINT! Lock into the Truth like a fish to the ocean. Release your image of the physical self. You are beyond that now. You are a spiritual being, a multidimensional being in the flesh as a beacon. You are invincible to negativity and so are all those around you (your family).
- Thank the Lord each day and night. Contact us for any help we may offer to you and your loved ones. We will speak with you again tomorrow at this time. "

I said, "Please tell me who you are."

The response was, "I am Kwan Yin."

1/28/94

Dear Kwan Yin, I hear and feel your presence. I invite you to please speak.

"My Child,

I am with you and I have wanted to speak with you since you left your driveway this morning. It is urgent that you hear and believe every word I tell you. You are a beautiful, most wonderful Child of God. You are childlike, as you should be. Ride the wings of your childlike manner and all good things will come to you. You know you are no longer afraid to speak, act or attempt anything. You know that it is yours because you have commanded it to be so. As I spoke with you this morning about the Jared situation, you handle the situation at no cost to you and Susan can handle getting people to the Flagler Dome. You do not offer conflict and you do not live in conflict for you know that is not of God. All will work out perfectly well. I am working with you every step, every moment with the project, and your center. There are others who are assisting you with your other projects such as the music ones with Donna and Frank. Trust both of them. Peace be with you as you learn of the Biogenic way of Life. I will be with you here as well. Your eyesight is fast becoming clearer, very shortly you will notice a difference. I am working with you on this matter as well. Do not ache inside for a child. You time will come, believe me, yes in this lifetime. No, you will not be too old my child. I am assisting you in rearranging the molecular structure of your womb. There are principles of Life that you are about to learn and that will assist you tremendously. Do not get frustrated. It is my honor to work with such an evolved human being. Praise God. Ask me for anything and it shall be done.

- Money for membership in DeBary Chamber of Commerce - Yes.
- Money for performing clothes - Yes.
- Money for PC and accessories - Yes.
- Money for your Reiki table - Yes.
- Money for new home - Yes.
- Money for rocking chair - Yes.
- Money for Hawaiian trip - Yes.

You have proved your faithfulness, faith and your love for God, self and neighbor. The mighty weight is now lifted from you...from your heart this moment. Sit back and allow me to do this.

Thank you,
Kwan Yin"

If you do not love yourself, what you think about yourself is revealed in your face, your eyes, your body language and your auric field. You will attract people in your life who are victimizers and manipulators (through the energy and thought forms you send out in your auric field) and you will not experience your highest good.

Each time you look at yourself in the mirror you will abuse yourself by what you perceive to be true, which is not. Your thoughts are things - energy. Your thoughts are power. Use your thoughts to your advantage to be successful, loving, loved, healthy and radiant. **Super Vita-Minds** are your partners for experiencing daily life at its fullest. Change one perception about yourself and you will see the miracles you have been overlooking for a long time. You will see how beautiful you are.

Brief Points of Chapter

- Thoughts are things. Thoughts are power.
- Thoughts are not neutral.
- The power of sitting in the seat of receptivity.
- The power behind intention.

Out of Time

Out of time
Not in it.
Out of Time
Not with it.
Beyond Space
Beyond limitation
Beyond all boundaries
One.
Gazing in the face
Of the ocean,
I can FEEL it
Hug every living thing
All AT ONCE.
Out of Time
Out of weigh-ti-ness
Out of fear
Out of fearfulness
Out of time
Is peaceful.
Out of time
Is stillness.
Out of time
Is Ecstasy.
Embraced by the
Arms of Timeliness
I know I am Total.
Embraced by the
Heart of timelessness
I am Unconditional Love
I know I AM
Out of Time.

Daya Devi-Doolin

CHAPTER ELEVEN

IMMACULATE CONCEPTION

Personal Journaling Concerning Intention And Its Application

February 3, 1994

I'd been prompted since the morning hours to sit down and write. At 4:00 PM, finally settled down in my bed to write as I was listening. Something very powerful, earth-shattering and Divine was about to blast its way through the Universe to me and I didn't know if I could handle the excitement I felt was waiting for me. But I guess I felt I was ready because it was about to happen. I didn't know if I was about to win millions of dollars, conceive a child, adopt an infant or be on Oprah Winfrey's show. Those were the things I related with this feeling I felt.

I said, "Peace Be with me," as I was listening and recording. "Thank you Father/Mother God." I turned off my beside light. I felt like I was about to have metaphysical surgery done or implantation of an embryo into my womb. It was very, very strange. I was asked to be quiet.

Conversations With Ascended Master Kwan Yin

As I sit crossed-legged in meditation pose, I feel the Presence of Ascended Master Kwan Yin. I asked Kwan Yin to make her presence known to me after I blessed and protected my being by the Light of Metatron. Kwan Yin (*See Glossary*) showed herself to me for the first time. She wore a blue satin cape and gown, brilliant royal blue. I said telepathically, "Oh, you are the one I saw before in the blue cape and gown the night before our ACIM meeting last year. She said, "Yes." She kissed me on my left cheek and my third eye.

She said to me,

> "You are about to give birth to a Holy Child. Time means nothing here so that's why I said about to give birth. Actually right now you are going to conceive him. You have told me you are in receptivity of conception and **So It Is!**"

As I had my right and left hand crossed over my heart, I sat and saw a beam of bluish white light come from her mouth into my ovaries and womb. I saw purple symbols flow out of her mouth within the beam of light.

Afterwards, I placed my hands lightly over my pubic area and asked Kwan Yin to please tell me what was happening. She said, "Conception has taken place now. Now all you have to do is wait."

February 4, 1994

I was reminded by Spirit to look at my blotter pad at the note I scribbled to myself February 1. It read, "A baby is come unto me." A Voice had merely whispered this information to me at 10:40 AM while at work on 2/1/94. Then I felt this energy in my solar plexus just explode all throughout my body!

After I composed myself, I was told to go outside of the building I was working in because the sun was out. I was to stand in the sun and feel its energy and so I did. While sitting on the railing of the little porch, I saw Tinke (read more about Tinke page 136) fluttering around in front of the sun. She was saying with such glee,

"See, I told you didn't I. I told you so!" I looked again to see if I really saw her and she vanished from my physical eyesight, so I knew to just feel her there and then I saw her again fluttering above and in front of me.

I started tearing because I knew I was not going to have a baby, I am having a baby - it was not to be in the future, but now. I had to refrain from allowing myself to cry because I didn't want people at work to think I was "unhappy" about something. I would not know how to explain anything about this wonderful news that I am to hold off about sharing. I might add here that I had always felt if Abraham's wife Sarah could have faith and have a child delivered unto her, so could I.

February 7, 1994

I remembered telling Chris as we lay in bed how my body was vibrating and tingling with such a powerful energy. It was electrifying.

February 9, 1994

Experienced spotting - pinkish blood. The same color and amount I saw when my first child was born twenty six years earlier. I know I am pregnant. I did not know before I woke up, but as I lay in bed relaxing while Chris was getting dressed, I mentioned to him how I felt so much energy tingling within me. I felt great, energized! He came over and bent beside me to receive what I was saying. He is wonderful how he pays attention to what I say even though I tease him about not listening to me when the TV is on. He is attentive and loving. I thought, this will be great for him! I'm going to test my urine with the pregnancy kit tomorrow morning first thing!

Home Pregnancy Urine test - negative. I told myself it was probably too early.

February 11, 1994

We had a facilitator come to our Reiki Healing and Training Center, Rev. Thomas "Sacred Bear" Young. After his three-hour presentation to registrants, he worked on and healed Chris. Chris had told him his third eye had felt like it was shut. Tom checked him out with his pendulum and energy work and said, "All centers were shut down." He opened all chakra centers on Chris and then worked with me.

I asked him, as he was working with me, if he would ask Spirit if there were an embryo. He found that there was and that a lost baby boy soul was still lodged within me. He helped me to place the baby boy in the hands of angels waiting for him at the heavenly doorway. Kwan Yin helped me through all of this as I was crying heavily. I had no idea that I still had sadness at the last miscarriage.

Tom smudged us with a sacred sage ceremony and protected our "home and healing center" with violet flame, silver, pink and blue light.

February 16, 1994

Kwan Yin, I await to write your message to me this Holy Day (Ash Wednesday). Thank you very much. Love, Daya

> "My Dear Little One,
> All is well for you. Do not worry or fret that what is, is not. You hold the truth in your womb. Tom Yong was there to help you to know this. He is an ambassador for me in his healing work. Allow the day to unfold its mysteries to you and be happy. Life is exploding within you. Remember your vision tapes and charts - do not fall away from them. Exercise is important now, squatting and walking. Feel how you feel and call on Tinke again if you wish. She's there for you. My blessings I leave with you. Kwan Yin."

Tinke - Please, speak to me! Daya

> "Ha-ha-ha-ha-ha-ha. Isn't life funny! I told you so, I told you so, I told you soooooooo!. Don't be afraid your heart will be broken again - all is well. You watch tonight. I will tell everybody in class that you

are pregnant, then you'll know for sure it's not baloney. I don't eat balony you know --Hee-hee-hee-heeeeee. Bye for now, see you tonight." (Tinke is one of my fairy friends. I had never had any experiences with fairies personally until now. She revealed herself to me one night at an intuition class I was taking with the La Rosa Wellness Center in Deland.)

February 18, 1994

I wrote and spoke to my embryo child and asked if I could come into its presence so I might hear what it had to say to its Daddy and me.

> "Mommy, I love you. I am not afraid anymore. Everyone in your class helped me to not be afraid. I was awfully afraid to come here, but I wanted to be here with you and Daddy for a long time. I'll be a quiet baby, a happy and healthy baby, and I'll also be a holy baby with my purpose. I am to lead people to the Light. You are a good Mommy, I'll be so glad to be in your arms and have you rock me in our new rocker. (*Referring to the 'Rocker' we could not afford but I bought anyway. Spirit had been very insistent that I do so. A way was made possible for me to do so by putting $4 - $10 down on lay-away every week.*) Thank you for picking it out with me Mommy. My work here will be very easy for you have paved the way for me with Daddy. I love your sweet music. I have always loved it. It makes me cry with joy to hear you sing. Will you sing to me a lot when I come?"

Our guest facilitator and friend, Rev. Carol Joan Garfinkel offered a wonderful seminar on Auras, clairaudience, clairsentience, and clairvoyancy. I learned from her that I have two guides and protectors over our home, belongings, and family, named Arias and Theisis. I invited Arias at that time to speak to me.

> "Daya My Child,

> You are wonderful to watch growing into your splendor of the Christ. It is my function to watch over you and your young ones. It is my honor to be of service to you at all times. You may call upon me for any help and I shall help you in any way I can. Be assured that I am with you and that you do see and hear me. The more you wish to come in contact with me, the clearer I will become to you.
>
> "Yes, you are with child and yes it is an Immaculate Conception as Carol Joan was speaking of. You must now consider that all you eat and desire to eat is of good consequence for your child. You have asked for a child and it is a real responsibility for you and Chris."

During an experiment that Carol Joan had led us through we were testing our clairsentience and clairvoyancy. I saw a baby crawling on the floor of our living room, which I **knew** was our baby, but allowed doubt to creep in.

I asked Arias if that was what I thought I saw crawling on the living room carpet.

> Arias replied,
>
> "Yes, but you were afraid to believe. Carol Joan told you to *Believe* you are hearing and seeing what you hear and see, for you are seeing, hearing and smelling."

Conversations with Ascended Master Ezekiel

February 20, 1994

Chris and I were working about the house organizing music, and paperwork. I felt this energy in and around my throat and heart chakra that was causing me to feel I was going to explode from the pressure of joy. I called to Chris to come to the kitchen and sit down with me.

I told him he had to get a notebook and write what I was about to channel. As soon as I sat down tears started welling up from within me with the energy of a being so powerful, strong and loving.

The voice, I was informed, was that of Ezekiel.

Ezekiel told me,

"Daya, through you it shall occur. I have been watching your work, watching you do the Will of God. Your faith will take you farther than you can imagine. You must continue to be open to the Will of the Lord, to His word and more and more doors will be opened. Ask and it shall be done unto you. We are here at your beckoned call. Your child is a holy child, protected by the Light and given to you by the Light. Your child will require nothing except your love. He knows the work he has to do, he is prepared and has been prepared for it. All will be and So It Is. I love you my children. I will inform you more of the work to come and your role in it. Do not be afraid that you are not hearing the right words. Do not doubt. It is my pleasure to be with you again. I am honored to speak with you. I leave you now in the name of the Lord Jesus Christ."

Ezekiel, I have a question or maybe more. Am I to say anything to anyone about the manner of conception?

"No."

Am I to tell anyone we are expecting?

"Only those who would be happy for you. Carol Joan and Connie are good starters. Donna and Patti are two you may tell, Gail and Merci later this week."

I know now that you have wanted to speak to me before on a few occasions lately, but I said no. Please forgive my ignorance. I know you do forgive me and that you have never condemned me for it. Thank you for coming to Chris and me. I am consumed with joy and the aftermath of your vibrations of Light.

I would ask of you to open the door to my physical sight, vision that I may see clearly without glasses now totally and completely. I ask if light surgery is necessary, then I open myself to it. Also, Ezekiel, would you be governing the project of the cassette on colors, chakras and musical notes?

"Yes."

Please inform me what to write for the meditation on each chakra color. I will be diligent until all that you wish to convey is written down for the growth of all that are led to purchase and listen to the cassettes.

"It shall be called "Chakra Symphony" as we learned today. Have them place their feet in red water. Add red food coloring to a clear glass bowl of water so they can actually feel the water and visualize the red. Have them absorb the water up through their toes, up to the first chakra, the root chakra.

Tell them they will be opening up their power center, their center of creation and regeneration. They will bring healing to their reproductive organs. Their sexual energy will be transmuted to a more creative energy on a higher level, not stuck on a lower plane.

Have them let the energy swirl around them at the base of their spine. This will clear away all problems and concerns of lack of money, lack in general and relieve back problems.

Then have them bring up red, blue, green, yellow, orange, purple indigo food coloring up through their centers. The other suggestions would be to buy swatches of colored felt to match what is needed.

Read this meditation to them:

As you place your feet in an imaginary stream, feel the vibration of the water. Feel your feet merge with the molecules of the water so you no longer feel separate from the water. Now you feel you and the water as one being. Now you will feel and see the (specific color) red water being drawn up into the cells of your toes. With each inhalation you will draw the water further up the legs to the base of the spine. Let it sit there in the pelvic area. Tune into it as it gives off rays of red light energy. Watch your emotions of anger turn into power, strength and creativeness. Roll with the energy, become one with it. Continue on with the process using each color."

February 26, 1994

Awakened by Spirit and listening (the time is 6:10 AM), I am to get up and write channeled information. I lie awake and feel I am not sleepy and affirm yes, I can do this (get up). I feel energy of the child bursting away in light rays, molecules moving, expanding and joining together the same way I felt and knew when Tyler was conceived. I knew the instant life had been created in me because I saw and felt a bright light in the form of a star fill up my uterus.

I am in the kitchen at the table feeling the movements of life in me growing. Now I know why I would get those waves of feelings that something precious, far greater than I could ever imagine was about to happen, manifest for us. They would sweep over me and fill me so much with bliss, love and beauty. I could only cry and sob with the touch of the love that flowed through me like electricity or a waterfall. The birds are chirping away - so happy and it's not even light out yet. I am to listen now - so...

I welcome all of you who are of the Light and permit whomever wishes to speak and identify himself to me in the name of the Father, Son and Holy Spirit.

"My Dear Light Child,

It is I, Ezekiel, who shall speak to you at this time. You are very obedient to the Will of the Lord. You glorify Him in all you do. You have asked and you have received and it shall be so much and more for you. As you experience more and more surrendering of the self, you will find it easier and easier to receive and do the Will of God. Your child is growing rapidly and yes it is finally here for you both. I enjoy your pictures on the wall. (I had placed pictures and my drawings of the birth, stages of pregnancy and one picture I had drawn of myself being pregnant. These

> included the details in my womb, adding Reiki symbols of energy going through my entire body into the child). That is good for you to do.
>
> The energy from these photographs helps you to see the reality beyond this world of illusion. Yes, the unseen world is reality and the seen world is illusion. But you can live in the seen world and exist in the unseen world at the same time. Parallel reality, multidimensional is all the same. Be not forgetful of being thankful at all times. Prayer is the link to us when you wish to do healing work. Continue to do so for your behalf and those who come to see you (for healing).
>
> Be not afraid that God's Will is not being done. You do not need to expect a certain outcome for anyone. Healing is taking place on all levels. When someone comes to you - they know this but you will need to remind them. Keep packing your thoughts in the right box.
>
> Go do something outrageous for yourselves today. Pick an animal to love. Walk sideways. Walk backwards and depend on each other to guide you backwards.
>
> This is all for now my sweet child. I leave you enclosed in peace. Ezekiel."

Conversations with Ascended Master, Mother Mary

Same day at 7:05 AM. I sense the presence of Mother Mary and ask if she wishes to speak too?

> "Yes. I have much to share. All is well for you my Dear Child. You are a radiant star among stars. You are already well known in your community of Earth. You shall become better known and this you sense but

do not know as yet. You and Chris are pillars for the planet as I have told you before. You are to be the next Mother and Father of the Planet. I know you do not see how this will be but that is not important - how? It is so.

Have Chris know not to FAINT and that we are working with him now for the work ahead of him. Remind him he is protected and that he is seeing the book closed on the unreal world. He cannot dwell where ego wishes him to dwell for very long anymore. He has been helped to go beyond. During the night we have all worked with him. You will see a different man but the same. We did some re-wiring, tightened some bolts and screws and gave him the go ahead. All is well. He can walk through any door that appears to be closed. He can imagine it opened, say 'open' or turn the knob and it shall be open for him.

God bless you all,
Mother Mary."

Brief Points of Chapter

- Be thankful at all times.
- The Unseen world is reality and the seen world is illusion.
- Parallel reality and multidimensionality is the same.
- Be not afraid that God's Will is not being done unto you.

Heaven is Now

Heaven is stillness.
Heaven is being here.
Heaven is lying here with you.
Heaven is knowing that I drink only holy water.
Heaven is knowing my food is holy.
Heaven is knowing I am blessed to eat holy food.
Who am I to think I can decree my food or anything as unholy or unnatural for me so that I can be overcome by the power I gave to it, to be scared by what I have mis-created in my mind?
Heaven is being and loving other holy people and knowing other holy minds like mine are blessing me.
Heaven is knowing everyone has a holy mind, even if they don't know it or believe it.
Heaven is knowing my womb is holy and nothing I can imagine can make it otherwise or take my peace away from me.
Heaven is knowing God has and always will take care of me.
Heaven is being married to Chris and loving him.
Heaven is being the divine mother of Tyler and Joseph.
Heaven is singing and knowing our music is healing to every one on every level.
Heaven is being loved by Chris, Ty and Joseph.
Heaven is knowing I AM One with God.
Heaven is knowing everyone is filled with ***God-ness****.*

Daya Devi-Doolin

CHAPTER TWELVE

WEEP NOT, NOR FAINT

Excerpts From My Personal Journal On the Power Of Intention And Its Application

March 3, 1994

Dear Kwan Yin,

I think that I am getting no support from Chris concerning our infant to be. I will not allow Chris to tell me that we cannot do this or cannot do that because I know I am not limited by anything or anyone unless I allow myself to be so. Please come and speak and comfort me, as I am feeling very sad about not having his cooperation and support.

Thank you.

"My Dear Child - Weep not nor faint. All is well, though you may not be aware of it at this time. He is just frightened that his hopes will be shattered and he is trying to protect himself by not feeling overjoyed. He will come around very shortly.

You have a question about where to put the crib that you just put on lay-away - the space for it is being provided for you. You will be moving and your bills will be paid. You will stay in the same location but a bigger place. I will continue to guide you. Your child is fine. Listen to him. Kwan Yin."

Finding Our Way Home

We found a home advertised for sale in June 1994. We put a down payment to buy it without knowing about the baby that was due to come to us in November 1994.

In August I had no longer felt the baby that was inside of me and I tearfully asked about it. I was told that it was spiritually implanted in me to grow and that now its place was to be physically implanted in another until its birth. I felt really stupid or that Chris thought that I was really out of my mind.

I had bought a rocker and crib for a baby that in his mind we had had no medical indication even existed. I said very strongly and with tears in my eyes, "Lord, you really have to show me I am not crazy! You told me to buy that crib and that rocker, now what am I to do with it?" Then I said, "Please forgive me for being angry with you."

March 18, 1994 (Saturday 5:30 PM)

I hear to write down my experiences -- something beautiful has been given to Chris and me. Back in February, Chris and I saw an antique store. We decided to stop the car one Sunday and go look around. We went to two antique stores in the same block and saw nothing that stood out, but I had the feeling we would know what we were looking for when we saw it.

We saw an antique store across the street and decided to go over there. There were at least six rocking chairs in the store. I tried them all and fell in love with only one. It was big enough for me to rock our new baby. Chris said we could not afford it and that was the end of that in his mind. I heard I was to buy it and that a way would be provided to do so.

I went back the next day (Monday) and did not tell Chris. I asked the salesperson if I could put $4 on the chair for lay-away. I told him I wanted to surprise my spouse with it as a baby gift and to let him know I was pregnant. Those were the words that were put into my mouth to speak, out of nowhere it seemed. Well, every week I put either $5 or $10 on the rocker faithfully. The salesperson noticed I was diligent in coming in with a payment. He told me that nobody else who has things on layaway comes in so regularly.

Well, I paid $10 that Thursday evening and got a call from them today. The salesperson, Robin, had called and said they made out a new receipt record for me and that the balance was no longer $152 but $122.

She said it's a gift for the baby, for both of us (Chris and me). I was all choked up inside. My friend Donna gave us the dream catcher that I had envisioned our child needed and now this beautiful gift of confirmation! It was almost too much love to handle.

March 30, 1994

> "I am here, your brother Ezekiel, to speak to you. Fret not my child. Everything is going fine here as well as for you too. Do not let dithers and smithers sprout about you. Yes, I do sound a bit British I say! The loftiness of what is happening within and without you is foreign, is it not? Be brave my child. Be brave my child. Let the mist fall from your eyes and face."

April 1994

I notice that I have a desire for strawberries and pickles, lots of them. The fresher the strawberries, the more I would have. I kept feeling wonderful but strangely so. There was some questioning of my ego mind.

May, 1, 1994

My friend, Carol Joan Garfinkel called me. She told me to keep a running journal of what is taking place and to do so until October or November, 1994. This is what else she told me:

- There will be a lot of surprises in store for me.

- Lots of etheric little beings around me and in our home.
- I see them all around Chris. (That much I already knew. I said is that possible? Did I really see a baby on his shoulder?) Yes.
- We will move from this home (Phonetia Drive) by October or November this year.
- I am discouraged about space for my center but I will be placed in larger quarters. (with a country décor theme.) I am to use things in a different way than they were meant to be used.
- There is an etheric being in me -- no within me--- she said that I am carrying an etheric baby within me, less dense than human, made of molecular gases. Other mothers (on the planet) and I have been impregnated, as Mother Mary has guided me. Other parents cannot procreate with each other in the etheric realm and so we are called to carry their beings for them. She said I would be taken into the etheric realm more and more to talk with my baby.

In August I knew the life form I had been honored to carry had been lifted up from me. I felt a little lost, to say the least. I was not attached to the loss, so I could go on with my life and not be stressed out, but I did wonder what was the point. What do I do now? I stopped the questions as soon I asked them.

Pretty soon I was absorbed in trying to buy that cute little house I mentioned earlier. It was not far from the house we had been renting for seven years. As you recall from a previous section, my friend Carol Joan had told us we were going to move to a new and bigger home in the same location.

We did not know when we saw the house advertised in the magazine that it was in a commercially zoned area. That is exactly what we had been looking for.

We wanted a place for our residence and for our healing training center and recording studio. We only learned about this information on our third visit to the place with the realtor. That's when she told us it was commercially zoned as well. She thought we had known already, but we hadn't.

Everything that Carol Joan had read to me psychically was happening. We put a down payment on the home in July, with the intention of moving in by September 1994.

One night while sleeping, a bright golden light awakened me and I heard my deceased father's voice. My father had passed away in 1979. He said, "Pumpkin, the house is yours. I am taking care of everything." I bolted right up in bed as if on a springboard. I started sobbing with such knowing. It was so powerful! I woke Chris up to share it with him.

We would come to understand what he meant by this. It was revealed quite by accident (this was not disclosed to us or the realtor) that the septic system was a health hazard and would not be passed by the health department for sale unless the owners put in a new one. The cost, $4,000.

We found out, not by our digging, that the well system had to be replaced by a new one, which was another $1,500 for the owners.

Another delay was faced when the underwriters had received our home inspection book and would not approve the loan because a few minor details like patching up old wood and replacing some molding that needed to be done. At the last minute, 4:55 PM, this was learned so our mortgage person just got a new underwriter who had no knowledge of our home inspection report.

At first the owners were not going to do any of the work, but they ended up doing so as my father had told me the house was ours and he was taking care of everything. The delays brought us to closing on the house December 8, 1994 instead of in September as planned.

In the meantime, before signing, we were contacted by the adoption agency we contacted *seven years ago* when we arrived in Florida. They asked if we were still interested in adopting. Stunned, we said, "Yes, of course." and then we were scheduled for a home interview. After the interview that Friday, we were called on Monday and told there was a baby just born who was interracial, healthy and newborn, which is what we requested on our forms seven years ago.

We were again asked if we were willing to continue onward and if so, they would schedule us for home study visits to see how the baby would fit into our lifestyles. (being musicians for example.)

Everything was going so fast! We found out later the caseworker wanted the baby to be settled as quickly as possible into his new routine. She had known we'd be the best parents for this baby. The adoption fee was not what we could afford and we told that to the agency. Our worker arranged to cut the fee in half for us and worked out a payment plan with us that we could live with.

There was smooth sailing until we found out we had to take a medical exam. Medical exams meant more money than we had planned. No one had told us about having to have a medical exam. We were slow moving after we found that out and almost decided against going ahead. Spirit had given us the "go ahead" and told us everything would work out fine.

I did some research on the costs of the four examinations we were required to have by the agency and found some large discrepancies in costs. At the local hospital, they wanted $125 for TB (Tine) test. This was just for one of us!

I called around that day to four different places and got quotations on the tests' costs. Finally I found a Family Health Center five minutes away from us that charged $10 for each of us. As you can figure, that is where we went. A total bill for each of was one we could more easily afford. Had we not been helped by Spirit and had faith, the door would have been closed to our baby and us.

Joseph, Father of Jesus

When we found out that we were actually going to be able to adopt a baby boy, we prayed together in bed. We asked the Lord what he should be called. Immediately I was shown Joseph and Mary before Jesus was born. I heard the words, "Joseph, Father of Jesus."

I was shown Joseph having just received the news of Mary being with child. I was told Joseph, the Father of Jesus was to be his name. I told Chris what I had heard and he said, "Yes, that's right." We decided his full name would be Joseph Paul (after Chris' middle name). We agreed, and said, "Yes, Joseph Paul Doolin! Yes!"

The Next Hurdle

The next hurdle that presented itself was as follows. Our adoption social worker knew we were planning to go to Philadelphia and Boston to see our respective parents and families for the Thanksgiving Holidays. I had asked her if it could be arranged to have our baby (she finally told us it was a baby boy) by November 18 or 19, as we were to leave for Philadelphia, November 20, 1994 (which was a Sunday). She said she would work on it. She said she had to do a statewide search for criminal records on us and a similar local search.

She called during this period and told me that the statewide search would take four weeks before they could determine if there were any criminal charges against us. She was heartbroken to give me this news. I started crying and she could hear it in my voice. I said, "All right", and thanked her for all the work she had done and hung up. I was near our bed and I got down on my knees and said, "Thank you Father for all You have done." I said, with all my breath and feeling, "Joseph Paul, if you want to be with us and go to Philadelphia and see your new family, then <u>you</u> have to make it happen now. I cannot do anything. It's all left up to you. God Bless you!" I got up from prayer and the phone rang. It was our worker on the phone again. She said, "You must have prayed, because my supervisor just told me to forego the statewide test and just do the local one. I'm sure it will be all right." I said, "You're right. I just finished praying," and I told her what I said in my prayer. I could feel she was teary-eyed.

The family health center that performed the tests on us had not sent in the reports on the day the agency needed them in order to process our new baby's arrival in our lives. That put off the time by two days. Now it was Wednesday and the nearby town had a severe flood so we could not go to pick up Joseph Paul for another day. The only day left to pick him up was Friday, because the foster mother could not be there Thursday, November 17, 1994. I knew everything would be all right, but we were still on pins and needles with excitement.

Chris' co-workers at the Maitland National Cash Register Office, (NCR) gave us a surprise baby shower before we left to pick up Joseph on Friday, November 18. We were very touched by their love for us and for what was happening for us. The shower was held at 11:30 AM, and we had to be at the adoption site by 3:00 PM to pick up Joseph.

I remember one of the things that our adoption agency worker said about Joseph when we asked her what he looked like. She said very strongly, "If my husband would allow me to, I would adopt him myself." That was perfect.

I saw Joseph in a vision, so I knew what he looked like but being in this world, I felt I did not know. We finally got to see and hold our immaculately conceived baby at 3:30 PM. The foster mother brought him into our worker's office. I held him first, then Chris. When Chris took him in his arms, Joseph raised his right hand as if to say, "Yes, I am home, I recognize you!" We were so happy and grateful.

The "Right" Parents

Our worker came to see us after a few weeks to see how we were settling in from our trip to and from Philadelphia and Boston. She told me that she had known all along that we were the "right parents" for Joseph. She shared with me how she always prays about each client and child before going any farther.

She told how she calls forth her intuition and follows it. Her supervisor had not wanted her to call us because of my age. She persisted in asking them to let her just interview us. Finally they gave in at the agency and said, "All right. Just interview them, but do not tell them we have a baby for them."

When she got back to the office, she told them again we were the right parents for Joseph and they still kept dragging their feet. They had not wanted us to be the parents because we were both over forty and they had a policy not to send babies out to parents over that age. However, they sent her out on her visit to us again. She later told me it was to see how fit we were. I have studied Yoga for over twenty years and she could tell I was very fit. In fact, she said I looked younger than my age.

She finally persuaded the adoption agency to let her do a home study with us and let us know there was a child available for us. She said she had pulled our names from a stack of papers a mile high. She remembered my name because it was so unusual and she said she remembered talking to me and I had such a beautiful, loving voice. She put two and two together and followed her instincts.

Now I realized what my Dad meant when he told me through spirit, "The house is yours and I am taking care of everything." He knew Joseph was coming into our lives and that he was going to need the new space. He helped us to get it. He knew we would need a nursery and it was provided for us. Joseph also knew he would need a place to play, live and grow and he had a part in shaping the events that took place to place him in our lives.

His physical parents conceived him on *Dec. 31, 1993* and we as etheric parents, conceived him that same day. He chose them as a vehicle to come through to this earth and chose us to grow with and love. My first son waited five years before coming to this earth. He knew he would have to do so at that time because a divorce was imminent from his father. Both Joseph and Ty are truly wise, brilliant and holy children! What a blessing they are to me and to the world!

Summary

What is ego? It is nothing but fear. It is simply a thought system we have mis-created. We have allowed it to separate ourselves from the Prime Creator (the thought of separation itself is an illusion). It keeps us a prisoner or slave to habits and personal thought patterns. It keeps us stuck in day-to-day life situations until we say, "Enough!, I surrender all illusions about myself to the Holy Spirit." Ego blocks us from accepting our good because we do not feel we deserve our good or deserve to be loved.

I am the Christ just as Jesus is and so are you. We are endowed with the Christ Consciousness just as He is endowed with it. Jesus is perfect. He always chose to listen to the Holy Spirit. He never allowed idols like anxiety, fear, jealousy, condemnation, judgment, fear of lack of money, distrust or dissatisfaction. to be his "Father." We choose these idols to be our "father" and then allow ourselves to be dissatisfied with the manifestation that these choices bring about. These choices keep us in a vicious cycle by choice.

Jesus was the Master of His physical life because He chose to think high vibratory thoughts that radiated in and without His being. He did it to show us that we too can be the Master of our lives. He did it to let us know we do not have to crucify ourselves every day with condemning thoughts about ourselves. It is a choice we make, to listen to the voice for ego or the Voice for God, the Holy Spirit.

Ego's use of guilt, anger, blame, judgment or criticism keeps us in a prison and what we give out we receive while in that prison.

Giving is having and giving is receiving. If we give out judgmental thoughts, critical thought, words or deeds, that is what we are proclaiming to manifest in our lives. That is what we will be receiving. You cannot give what you do not have. You cannot give love if you are unloving; therefore you will not receive it or know that you have truly received it from Christ on a parallel reality. What you give out comes back to you magnified.

We block the channel of good from coming to us because of our disbelief that it could happen. We would be able to see the miracle before our eyes if we were willing to change our perception about what we think we see. Changing our perception of what we see shows us the miracles that are before us.

We could ask the Holy Spirit to reveal the true meaning to us of what we see or experience. Instead of seeing ourselves as limited (ego's view of ourselves) and lacking, unhealthy, getting old, weary and unloved we could turn those thoughts over to the Holy Spirit and begin to see ourselves as totally whole, safe and secure.

The vibration of these words alone such as, I am whole, safe and secure, will make it so. I am my perfect weight. Saying, "I have more than enough money to have fun, travel and serve others", will heal you immediately. The Light from these words focuses energy into the dark cells of our being and irradiates love everywhere, within and without. It allows us to walk on water (turmoil in your life), as did Jesus.

The next and final step is to be totally **GRATEFUL** for everything you see around you happening, **in** your life and **without**. That is how you change things, by being grateful, not by being critical or judgmental of anything or anyone. Once you are grateful for the space in your consciousness that you have graduated to, you can move into an even more unlimiting consciousness and become more of a servant to mankind on an unconditional level. Being grateful de-crystallizes all negative energy blocks on a cellular, emotional/mental and spiritual level throughout the entire body.

When we put ego in its rightful place, which is that of a teacher instead of our Creator, we will automatically get off the treadmill of "I hate myself, I hate my life, I hate the world." consciousness. We can say, "Thank you, ego, for letting me know I do not want to be in this space anymore. Thank you for showing me there must be something better for me than this mentally, emotionally, physically debilitating space that I have mis-created. I am grateful that I can change. I am grateful I am Master of my Life!"

In this book, I have written about the power we all have behind our intentions and thoughts. I have explained how thoughts are things and how to use them to our advantage. I have shown the importance of changing our perception about ourselves in order to see the miracles that are before us in parallel reality. I have given examples on applying the techniques. It has been my intention that you become empowered enough to know you can change your life, relationships or any illness, simply by the positive way you feel about yourself and by believing that you can do so.

You can come to realize you are a beautiful, loving being. You deserve all the love that is meant for you to have.

I have shared with you how, by your faith in a Higher Power and the energy you put behind your faith, you can give your goals the power to manifest boldly and securely in your life.

What is there that is difficult to manifest in our lives? Nothing, if we but believe that it is possible.

It has been my personal intention to sit in the seat of receptivity of my highest good. Part of that intention includes having beautiful holy children, a beautiful place to live, a flourishing metaphysical healing center and church that touches the lives of others, a fantastic recording career that uplifts thousands. I intend to keep sustaining and nurturing the love of myself, developing deep abiding friendships. I intend to write the necessary books, articles and newsletters that I am guided to write.

Believe that you can make your life a blessing for all that come in contact with you as well. Make your intention a powerful one. Make your intention to Love Yourself as powerful as you can make it.

Do everything you can possibly do to have fun while doing this. Let your joy **Be** in the doing for yourself and celebrating yourself. Bless yourself every single day and give thanks always for the beauty within you. My love is with you as you begin to look past illusions from the "**outside in**".

When you totally and completely love yourself, there is absolute trust and faith in all your decisions, because you are recognizing the God-Self that you truly are. Your God Self can make no mistakes because you are operating from Love and Love cannot but be Loving.

I have shown you many tools you can use so that you can now begin in this moment saying and knowing, "**I Love Me!**" Watch the door of everything begin to open itself to you and the many mansions beyond it that are there for you to explore.

Be prepared for the spiritual facelift that is the side effect of absorbing **Super Vita-Minds** into your spiritual bloodstream. You will become a changed person. You will be the person that no longer needs to say, I Hate You...To Yourself!

Don't forget, take one - two caplets of **Super Vita-Minds** and call me in the morning! I Love You!

Brief Points of Chapter

- Ego is fear. Ego is our teacher not our Creative-Mind.
- Sit in the seat of receptivity while your good is being shown to you.
- Follow intuition and visions to your good.
- Make your intention a powerful one.
- Let your joy be in doing for yourself.
- Recognize your God Self and celebrate it.

APPENDIX i

In this section of the book, I have included some metaphysical truths that have helped shaped my spiritual life and purpose on this planet. You will also find some worksheets and pages for you to journal in as you read this book and jot some thoughts down in it while you read. I do not want you to have to go looking for a piece of paper and become distracted.

Also in this appendix section will be meditation techniques, an exercise on forgiveness and an essay on manifesting your good. Chris and I have used these successfully in our seminars and workshops. There are books included for recommended reading. They have a deep abiding place in the cupboard of our hearts as I hope they will find in yours.

APPENDIX ii

*A*CCESSING Your Good

This article is a summary of a booklet entitled, **The Manifestation Process. (10 Steps to the Fulfillment of Your Desires)** by John Randolph Price, A Quartus Publication. *(See References).*

I have found this little booklet very helpful in my life and in sharing it with others through my workshops, seminars and lectures. If you practice or go through the techniques you will find your life heading in the way you wish to see it too. Perhaps you could have a friend do this with you or a loved one who shares your dreams.

Step 1 Principle of OPENING YOUR HEART. This is based on opening your heart and mind to a spiritual nature. It is tuning into that Presence and Power of God within you. If you do not have this, you will be working with mind power that offers different results. To get the full impact of the awareness of the Presence, you have to be willing to FEEL it. Look within and feel it.

Step 2 Principle of CHOOSING. Get the thought of what you want as clear as you can. Make a list of what you want, put it in writing and understand that this is choosing.

By choosing you begin to exercise dominion in all of your life. Spirit will speak to you through intuition, guiding you to choose even greater experiences. All the good that God has for us has already been given to the Reality within us, our Higher Self. We have every thing right now, but we have to claim it.

Step 3 Principle of ACCEPTANCE. Spirit cannot make the gift available unless you accept it. Only that which you are willing to accept will be yours. All God's gifts to you are first in thought form and when we accept these thought forms a pattern of expression of that thought form is established in consciousness. Once you choose what you want, you accept it mentally and with the fullness of your feeling nature.

Step 4 Principle of HAVE. When you accept something, you have it even if it is first in the invisible form. When your consciousness accepts that you have accepted it, then it shifts from a sense of need to one of Have. Joel Goldsmith says in his book, "By acknowledging that we HAVE, we shall demonstrate HAVE." Move away from "need" to knowing you already have and you shall have it happen for you.

Step 5 Principle of VISUALIZATION. Through the power of creative visualization, you are in the closest proximity to the activity of God-Mind. This power is called imagination. Through imagination, we have the power to change misfortune into favorable situations, disease into health, unhappiness into joyousness.

This is controlled mental picturing. It's not daydreaming. See yourself having the fulfillment of your desires in the present moment. Always work in the NOW. One way that helps is to look at what you are wearing prior to visualizing. See yourself doing, being, having and enjoying your good as an accomplished fact. Do not see yourself trying to arrange things, like a loan for a car. See yourself as driving your friends and taking trips. Add sound, color and dimension. Watch the people involved with you.

Step 6 Principle of LOVE. Be sure to love what you are seeing. Generate the warm and beautiful feeling of love and let it radiate through the images in your mind. Love is the power behind the whole thrust of creation. Through the love vibration, you unite the conscious, subconscious and super conscious phases of your mind, and you embody the pattern that represents the fulfillment of your desire.

Step 7 Principle of the SPOKEN WORD. Words that we speak cause a vibration in the universal energy field. The effect of that vibration will return to us in direct accordance with the nature of the word. Your word cannot return to you void. You let your good come forth and you firmly declare IT IS DONE. The Universe says AND IT IS SO.

Step 8 Principle of SURRENDER. It means we totally and willingly accept The Truth, the Way and the Life of our Higher Consciousness. Let God work out the how and the details. We must get out of the way of trying to manipulate our good and how it is to come. You will know you have surrendered when you are no longer anxious, concerned, worried or demonstrating negative energy.

Step 9 Principle of GRATITUDE. Have a joyful heart filled with praise and thanksgiving, an overwhelming sense and feeling of gratitude because you KNOW that your problems are solved and your needs are met.

The **SECRET** -- be grateful while your good is still invisible! There must be a deep feeling of gratitude in your heart. Gratitude releases a dynamic current of spiritual energy to go before you to exert a mighty influence in your world. It eliminates the negative patterns in the subconscious caused by ingratitude.

Step 10 Principle of ACTION. Move into action. God's law works through you. Do whatever it is that intuition guides you to do, NOW! Always listen to that inner feeling for guidance. God can and will meet our needs. We have to act faithful, be faithful and work as if we have what we desired.

Move from fear, doubt and worry. Clean the house, office, car, yard, like it has never been cleaned before or complete a project you've been putting off. Ask the Holy Spirit what you should do next? Listen as you are being still and *Act*. Your actions will eliminate your fears. Follow each lead and direction God gives you.

You can make your own personalized tape yourself with your own voice. Put some soft background music behind your voice for added impact to your subconscious mind.

APPENDIX iii

START GIVING YOURSELF PERMISSION TO LOVE YOURSELF TODAY!

Fill your name in the blanks and you can also add statements yourself.

I, ____________________give myself permission not to use my body as a battleground anymore.
I, ____________________give myself permission not to abuse my body anymore.
I, ____________________give myself permission not to hate myself anymore.
I, ____________________have no reason to hate myself or punish myself.
I, ____________________am a perfect being, a loving being, and a forgiving being.
I, ____________________give myself permission to be lovable to myself and do fun things for myself.
I, ____________________no longer plague myself with hateful thoughts.
I, ____________________sow loving thoughts to my body, mind and heart.
I, ____________________love my hair, my face, my teeth, my chest, my breasts, my abdomen, my thighs, my arms, my family, husband, wife, brother, etc.
I, ____________________listen to my Comforter on what to do, say, think and feel at all times.
I, ____________________no longer deny I hear my Comforter.
I, ____________________no longer want to deny that I hear His Voice telling what His Will is for me.
I, ____________________no longer need to be dissatisfied with me.
I, ____________________no longer need to be dissatisfied with my life.
I, ____________________no longer need to drown myself in despair.

I, __________________can no longer not listen to the Holy Spirit because I know IT is my Presence.
I, __________________am at one with my ideal health and weight.
I, __________________am at one with my ideal job, husband, wife, child, etc.
I, __________________no longer need to smoke, overeat, lust, be jealous, idolize money, sex, clothes, people or other things.
I, __________________am at Peace.
I __________________am still.
I __________________am not alone.
I __________________am strong in the Lord! All is Well!
I __________________am enfolded by Spirit of Truth at ALL Times!
I, __________________am Forgiven and I forgive myself for believing I was weak and unworthy of LOVE!

APPENDIX iv

Forgiveness Exercise

This exercise was designed by Chris and myself for one of our study groups in order to help them to apply the message of Chapter 9 of **ACIM**. I share this with you now.

If I were to forgive someone, who is the first person that comes to mind? Is it myself or someone else?

Why do I need to forgive him/her?

What does it mean if I forgive them or myself?

If I forgive them or myself, then this means I have to__________
____.

Please circle one or all (event, person, situation, myself, etc.) and give your own reason(s) below for not forgiving. Use more space as needed. Then write, I now decide to forgive (name) because I want to know peace, freedom, oneness, joy and love. I desire to be free of the pain of unforgiveness.

What would happen to me if I decided to totally and unconditionally forgive myself or ___________________________(name of person)?

I now choose to forgive____________________________________
__________________________________, because I would like to be forgiven and freed from the prison I have built around myself and the person I would not forgive. Forgiving them means that I ______
____
______________________.

List all those whom you would like to forgive and then forgive them.

List all those whom you wish would forgive you and for what.
Know that in God's eye, you have never done anything to be forgiven for because He created you perfect like Himself. Only you have thought yourself imperfect because of how your ego perceived itself.

JOURNALING PAGE

JOURNALING PAGE

JOURNALING PAGE

Soft As Air

(The next two poems were written for my first son, Tyler when he was 5 yrs. old.

I love your little kisses
That feel as soft as air.
I love your little squeezes
That show me how you care.
I love your little hands of pink
That feel as soft as puppy paws,
I love your little, big brown eyes
That say I love you,
Just because!

Daya Devi-Doolin

Mommy, I Can't Hear God's Voice

Mommy, I can't hear God's voice.
Why doesn't He talk to me?
He talks to you, and tells you things,
But He forgets I'm me.
Soon, you'll hear His voice, my son
That's deep inside of you.
Soon you'll find the joy inside
And know that you are One.
He's in the wind
And the quiet lake,
And the beautiful butterfly.
He's in the kiss when you kiss my cheek
And the hug that makes me cry.
He's in the toad that you
Found today
And the squirrel you
Found to feed.
He's in the love that you
Shared with me
When I held you on my knee.
He's in the sparkle
Folks see in your eyes
That brightens up their day.
He's in the twinkle that lights
Up your smile,
That carries you on your way.
Mommy, I **can** hear God's voice
And He does talk to me.
He sings to me and He tells me things
And He says that you love me!

Daya Devi-Doolin

Laughter In The Wind

I hear laughter in the wind
Children's voices
Clamoring with glee
Like sea gulls over a feast of oysters
and clams.
The essence of their joy
Wraps around my heart
As an umbilical cord connects a baby
To Life.
And now,
I too am laughing!

Daya Devi-Doolin

You Are My Light in Shining Armor

(Written for my dear husband, Chris.)

You are my light in shining armor
Always lighting up my way
Filling up my days with laughter
Filling all my nights with play.
Words that cause my cells to giggle,
Words that touch my very soul
Lighting all my darkened pathways
Causing me to thirst for more.
I'm in need to be reminded
So you tell me everyday,
Just how much you really love me
Even when you're far away.
Words that tell me I am your You-ness
And I am the Holy One;
Blending with my I AM presence
Sharing with the Father's Son.
Yes, you are my shining armor.
Yes, you are my You-ness too;
Yes, you are the light within me
That brings light to me and you.

Daya Devi-Doolin

"I Can See Things Differently"

I see there is only perfection in this tree.
How could I think there could be anything less
With me?
There is perfection in all my affairs.
There is perfection in me.
I see there is only perfection in this ocean.
How could I think there could be anything less
With me?
There is perfection in all my affairs.
There is perfection in me.
I see there is only perfection in that sea gull.
How could I think there could be anything less
With me?
There is perfection in all my affairs.
There is perfection in me.
I AM that tree.
I AM that ocean.
I AM that sea gull; so I AM perfect too.
There is only perfection in all of me and in all of You.
And That's The Truth!

Daya Devi-Doolin

Meditation

According to Richard Gerber, M.D., author of **Vibrational Medicine**, "A very simplistic and powerful method of opening, activating and cleansing blockages in the chakras is through the techniques of meditation. Although meditation is sought by many as a source of relaxation, it is much more than that. In addition to providing relaxation to the body, meditation opens the mind to the energies of the Higher Self. It helps to clear the mind of day-to-day concerns of the earthy personality, and allows higher information to be processed through the individual's consciousness. Most forms of meditation do this to some degree or another. However, certain meditative techniques are more powerful than others in accelerating this process of inner communication." I have included two methods below but keep in mind, there are many forms that allow you to process information from your Higher Self. They clear chakra blockages, allow answers to pour forth regarding your questions and allow gradual changes in the energy anatomy to take place.

Meditation #1

This is a meditation that came into my possession and I do not have the person or book that it came from so I cannot give due credit. At the time I received it I had no idea I would be writing this book.

"I open myself to the greatest healing powers of the universe - that all who come in contact with me might be healed, within and without, by the mere presence, by the mere thought, by the mere touch of the garment, for I AM.

I would sleep and rest my being, and I would relieve myself from the burden of learning in other dimensions that the rest might be complete. My energy centers would be closing that I would be allowed complete and total rest of my being.

I open myself to total and complete rest of the entire being. Light comes through the top of my head through a little opening.

Its color is pink. It fills every part of me, down through my arms, hips and legs and through my feet. From top to bottom I am filled with this pink color, love from the universe. The spirit wind blows ever so gently on the pink color slowly moving the ripples of pink massaging my entire body. There are angels on either side of me as I sleep that place clouds around me like my mother would nurture me. They make wonderful soothing sounds, lovely sounds for my being. They make the sound of the universe.

I allow myself to release that I might be in total surrender. I totally and completely surrender. My child within is content, restful and happy until morning. There is nothing I need do. I AM."

This passage has always helped me if I were having a difficult time getting to sleep. I have shared it with many clients who have gotten relief from sleeplessness. It is suggested that you record the above meditation on a tape and play it for yourself as you are resting in bed.

Meditation #2

Inhale three deep inhalations and exhalations. Each exhalation, draw in the abdomen as far as you can letting go of all Carbon Dioxide, tension, stress and fears. On the next breath, inhale and hold the breath. Look into the quietness with your third eye (inner eye) all around and inside your body and mind. You will feel your rhythm spiraling. You will get in touch with your molecular pattern, you will see and feel your molecules of light pulsating. You will be merging with Your Self, your God Self. Release the breath effortlessly when ready to inhale again. Repeat this process for as long as you feel the need, anytime of the day or night.

APPENDIX vi

Glossary of Natural Healing Modalities

Some of these healing techniques have been around for thousands of years and have been known to increase the vibrational frequency of our chakra centers (wheels of light) and aura assisting us in total and complete healing.

There are many alternative natural healing modalities available to us. These modalities are here to best suit our purposes, according to our belief that there has to be a better way for us to recover from spiritual, mental, emotional or physical illness.

Below is a brief description of a few alternative healing modalities which you could choose to use in addition to any allopathic medical treatment you may now be using. They can enhance and speed up your recovery. We use several of these methods with our clients and there have been excellent results.

For those of you who are not familiar with the works offered for drug-free healing here are some brief descriptions that will work in line with a change in your thoughts. These processes can work for AIDS, CANCER or other terminal illnesses, psychological, mental or physical problems. Some have not been proven according to medical science's satisfaction but they have worked for the client.

Aromatherapy

Aromatherapy utilizes flower petals, roots, barks, leaves and oils from plants. Pure essential oils are not diluted and are very powerful and effective in raising the hertz frequency to that of normal frequency and vibration. They can be used for burns, bruises, skin irritations, leucocyte production, respiratory problems, intestinal disorders and emotional or mental problems. The oils go into the system within 3 seconds and into the blood stream with three minutes.

Reiki

Reiki translates to mean Universal Life Force Energy. It was rediscovered by a Buddhist Monk by the name of Dr. Mikao Usui. A Reiki Practitioner will administer this energy for a client to utilize as his higher self sees the need. Normally, the client undergoes three 1 hour sessions, and then it is determined if more sessions are necessary and/or how frequently. The energy unblocks deep-seated emotional, mental or physical problems. A typical Reiki session brings about spiritual clarity, calmness, release of pain and stress. Unwanted habits can sometimes be alleviated, such as smoking and drinking. Rev. Daya Devi-Doolin, B.Sc., R.M.T. (Reiki Master/Teacher)

Rebirthing (Conscious Connected Breathing)

Rebirthing is a form of integrative breath-work. It is simply a breathing technique for greater well being of body, mind and spirit. It was re-discovered by Leonard Orr in 1975 but different forms of conscious breathing have been practiced in many cultures throughout history as a means of purification and self-awareness. During a rebirthing session a Rebirther guides you to a fuller, freer, more energetic breath. This produces a physiological change that increases energy, reduces stress and cleanses and purifies. It also creates an altered state, which allows old thought patterns to release thereby dissolving and healing trauma. Sondra Ray and Leonard Orr have co-authored the book on **Rebirthing in the New Age.** Rebirthing is merging the inner and outer breath to experience fullness of divine energy in the physical body. It's a release of all your resistance to life. - Rev. Daya Devi-Doolin.

Whole Light Fusion

"Whole Light Fusion is a system that teaches you how to attune your consciousness to the universal gateway (zero point) in which light condenses into matter. Whole Light Fusion is a synthesis of breath and energy work, which provides a resistant free way to conduct this vital life energy through your breath. You will learn how to radiate life energy through your hands, and to share this healing force with others." I. Jared Rosen, Developer of Whole Light Fusion Life Energy Systems, Marin County, CA.

Past Life Regression

"Through the emotional feelings and body sensations associated with an identified present life problem, the client is prompted to locate the source or cause of the problem. This leads to the discovery of a pain-filled memory in a past life. The client, in the personality of the past life character, is guided through the traumatic episode in the lifetime, and finally through the death experience. The therapist assists the client in resolving any remaining emotional issues, any unfinished business in that life, and to integrate the experience into the present life situation. The past life character, as a spirit, moves away from the body and the death scene and fully into the Light." - William Baldwin, DDS, Ph.D. (See Recommended Reading)

Ro-Hun Therapy

"Ro-Hun Therapy is an integrated, energy based method of healing. The process utilizes the energy systems of the client in creative interaction with the energy field of the therapist to bring about deep and insightful change. In so doing, the individual is then able to sustain a positive and productive perspective in his or her life. The Ro-Hun therapy consists of three two-hour sessions with one or more follow-ups, if needed." The Patricia Hayes School, McCaysville, GA 30555. Gloria Andrioli is a Ro-Hun Practitioner in Lake Mary, FL.

Colonic Hydrotherapy

A Colonic therapist is licensed to aid the individual in flushing the entire intestinal tract (large and small intestines) with the use of water and the right amount water pressure to evacuate debris and promote a healthy environment for digestion, assimilation and evacuation to take place.

Naturopathy

Practitioners utilize herbs, sunlight, hydrotherapy, diet, homeopathy, exercise and fasting to bring about healing. They prefer to stay away from surgery and drugs, used only as a last resort. You may wish to check out *Homeopathy* on your own.

Rolfing

Developed by Ida Rolf in the 1930's in the U.S. Based on the concept that gravity creates distortions which occur throughout to the skeletal muscles. Rolfing helps the posture and brings balance to the body.

Feldenkreis

A great stress releasement technique. The lessons lead to better posture and balance.

Massage Therapy

There are sports massage, Swedish massage, aromatic massage and self massage. Aromatic massage is aided by the use of essential oils such almond, olive, rosemary and lavender to name a few. These methods aid in reducing stress, pain and healing the body of trauma to organs and tissues.

Reflexology

Relieves the body by removing crystalline deposits from meridians (nerve endings) of the feet through the therapist's using deep pressure massage. A form of reflexology massage has its early origins in China and is known to have been practiced by Kenyan natives and North American Indian tribes for centuries. Reflexology helps to activate the body's natural flow of energy by dislodging the collected deposits. *(See References)* .**Toxicless Diet,** Patricia Bragg.

Hydrotherapy

One of the oldest forms of medicinal healing involves using water in various ways. Hot and cold baths or showers using aromatic oils on the skin beforehand encourage an increase in blood circulation and relaxation. For muscle aches and pains you can use apple cider vinegar or Epsom salts.

TRANSFORMATIONAL AND SPIRITUAL GROWTH

If you are interested in Transformational and Spiritual Growth you may choose to select an Alternative Holistic Healing Clinic or Practitioner in addition to your medical program for a complete healing. You may find personal growth and spiritual training enhanced by doing so. Use your own intuition. We are here to help and we can also refer you to other alternative organizations or practitioners who have your best interest at heart.

The Doolin Healing Sanctuary
Directors: Revs. Chris and Daya Devi-Doolin
P.O. Box 4267
Enterprise, FL 32725-0267
(888) 369-9884 Email: cdoolin@bitstorm.net
Usui Reiki Classes & Therapy I, II, and III Degree, Past Life Regression, Group & Indiv. Rebirthing, Meditation classes, **ACIM** Study Groups/Facilitators, Spiritual Counseling and free introductions to Whole Light Fusion, Outreach Programs and special events.

Free Candlelight Healing & Metaphysical Church Services are held the first Sunday of each month, from 6 PM to 8 PM. You may write to us for a free sample of The Holy Instant Newsletter or subscribe to the newsletter.

Graduates of our Reiki Training and Healing include Reiki Master-Teachers: Rev. Carol Jo Garfinkel, Robert and Iris Reynolds, Diane (Gabrielle) Fisher, Louis Albert Endara and Zoila D. Clement.
First Degree Graduates are: Beth Morgan, Eddie Morgan, Chris Doolin, Donna Gwaltney, Patricia Collins, Robert Reynolds, Iris Reynolds, Madeline Grovesnor, Sammie Meikle, Tyler Mitchell, Gail Fleming, Regina Martin, Dianna Russo, Kevin Reynolds, Jessica Russo, Danielle Cruse, Tyler Reynolds, Charles Shugart, MaryAnn

Krenzke, Frances Gilbert, Sallie Brown, Jean Campana, Pedro Fernandez, Lydia Bandini, Raquel Sparks.
Second Degree Graduates: Sammie Meikle, Tyler Mitchell, Madeline Grovesnor, Louis Albert Endara, Rev. Carol Jo Garfinkel, Diane Fisher, Bob and Iris Reynolds, Beth Morgan, Gloria Andrioli, Charles Shugart, Kathy Hade, MaryAnn Krenzke, Lydia Bandini.

The First Degree graduates of Rev. Carol Jo Garfinkel are: Kalman Tornick, Jackson Pitts, April Townsend McMahon, Karen Dell, Sandra J. Short, Carmen Velez, Lin Curtiss, Cathy Parish, Norma Young; Second Degree: Barbara Bordeaux, Ruby Vega, Jackson Pitts.

The First Degree graduates of Bob and Iris Reynolds are: Patricia Hefley, Jane Hires, Kathy South; Second Degree: Dianna Russo, Patricia Hefley, Kathy South, Jack Lowe and Daisy Whitfield.

It is an honor to have shared this sacred alternative method of healing with all of you. Congratulations and Best Wishes! May you continue on with your life's purpose as a Light Worker and stay plugged into the Source!

GLOSSARY

Ascended Masters - They are messengers of God from the Fifth and Sixth Dimensions to guide and to remind us of our true nature. They all work under the guidance of Ascended Master Sananda also known as Jesus Christ. To name a few, they are Archangel Michael, Gabriel, Kwan Yin, Kuthumi, St. Germain, Mother Mary, Serapis Bey, Ezekiel, El Morya, Raphael, and a Host of others. These Beings are also known as the White Brotherhood because of the vibratory energy of their spiritual bodies and consciousness. They are with us to provide guidance, healing, wisdom, protection and love. We can access their power and protection just by saying something like, "I am guided and protected by the Light of the White Brotherhood." You can be specific by invoking the violet flame of St. Germain to dissolve all unforgiving issues in your life. Use their protection or the White Light protection before you meditate. You may read more in the **Law of Life Vol. I & II.** (*See References*).

Atonement - It is a pure act of sharing, correcting and the undoing of error.

Attack - The belief that we can be attacked. Blame, guilt, anger is thought possible.

Aura - The body of energy that layers itself around our physical body for protection, illumination and health. Aura means life.

Body - The ego abuses the body through emotions of rage, anger, doubt, body thoughts of anxiety, and attack thoughts. It sees the body as tense, anxious, stiff, tired, weak, drained, lacking energy and prone to weakness or disease. The Holy Spirit loves the body and energizes it as a thought crystal of living love energy. The Holy Spirit sees the body as full of life, vitality, energy, zeal, strong, healthy and unstoppable, but knows that we believe otherwise.

Cause and Effect - All that we do is the result of what we think, believe and intend. The effect is the manifestation of our thoughts in action.

Cellular Transformation - When one understands the concept of God and the life force of the universe, then the merging of the Holy Spirit or Higher Self and the physical body with the other seven bodies of the aura takes place. When this takes place it ushers us into higher frequencies of Light, higher dimensions and transformation takes place.

Chakras - Chakras are electromagnetic wheels of light that circulate up the energy field of our aura. Aura means life. The aura mirrors the flow of life around a person. It is controlled by the chakras. The frequency of the chakra spin determines the color of a particular chakra and the health of those surrounding cells and organs. Our thoughts, attitudes and beliefs govern the health or lack of health of our chakra centers. Chakras have a specific color, sound and frequency. These all monitor the auric field.

Channeling - Receiving guidance, knowledge, directions for spiritual growth by becoming an open vessel for Spirit to speak through and to you. The information could be for planetary growth, individual or group growth. One should get centered by going into meditation, call forth the White Light of Protection to encircle you and invoke the presence (singular or plural) of White Brotherhood Council to speak through and to you. Always give thanks for the messages. *(See Recommended Books **Bridge Into Light** for more specific details.)*

Co-creator - Humanity is the co-creator with God. We have come to earth to remember this.

Consciousness - A state of awareness, a level of vibrational frequency we are living in. I am that I Am. That which I think is that which is. Life is consciousness. All life is consciousness. Consciousness is aligned with being centered. Plants, animals, humans, all living creatures embrace it. As far as humans, we have an awareness of the I AM PRESENCE, Truth, a vibratory rate of frequency. You can have a low frequency vibration or a highly vibrating frequency according to the thought forms you entertain on a daily basis. Thoughts of low energy base keep you depressed. You choose these. Thoughts of a high vibratory rate are positive and keep you happy, healthy, vibrant and youthful. You choose these as well.

Ego - Ego is illusion. It wants you to believe that you are separate from God and the Universe. It is fear. It is highly developed to keep itself unknown to you to undo what God has created. It attempts to keep you from the Light, from remembering who you really are.

Fear - Belief that negativity exists and we are separate from God.

Fifth Dimension - Earth and humanity are going through an evolutionary cycle to begin their journey into the Fifth Dimension. The soul will have been given direction to participate and move forward to participate in the lessons that build its "character," thus raising its frequency for entrance into the higher realms of Light.

Forgiveness - Our release from guilt and anger. Giving up hate, anger for the gift of love. Forgiving enables you to step through the portal that ushers you through a higher frequency of thought manifestation.

Healing - The removal of All Fear. The giving up fear thoughts to the dominion of Love. Healing is the forgiving of negative emotional, physical, and mental tension around the issue of ourselves.

Holy Spirit - The Voice for God within us that responds to our call for a renewal of mind and healing. The Executive Will of God directs us from within.

I AM - Is the life principle in your body. The creative word to all that manifests for you. It calls forth life into manifestation.

Illusion - the belief that ego is the father and not God.

Judgement - An attribute of ego. "In God there is no judgement nor conflict." **ACIM**

Light - Light is the presence of all color and all sound. We all have but to meditate on the Light within us and we will lift ourselves out of darkness and negativity that surrounds us. Light contains everything we could desire for change and prosperity. We have to choose to go the Light or be swept off the face of the Earth. The Light vibration will not be able to be tolerated by dark energy forms like fear, guilt, hate and evil. Our Earth is travelling toward a continuum where nothing but Light, which is peace, can exist. It may come about anytime now. When your vibration rate equals that of ultraviolet, then you enter the sixth dimension. Beyond that, one becomes a member of and assumes a position on the Tribunal Council of the Galactic Command. They are one with Light.

Metaphysical - That which is happening beyond the physical realm, that which we cannot see with our five senses.

Multidimensional - We have many layers to our physical and spiritual self. They exist on the third dimensional level and beyond. When we decide to be of One Mind with God we can experience all that goes with it.

Parallel Reality - We are used to seeing with our five senses. When one accepts that there are other possibilities of realities, he will "see" other worlds parallel with our earth. His soul will begin to vibrate at a higher level and his consciousness will be raised and united with higher levels of thought form. All we have to do is change our perception. Choosing to move from illusion to truth will bring automatic sacred information to you from other worlds.

Revelations - When one's soul merges with its Higher Self, it is allowed to receive transmissions and revelations for its highest good.

Sickness - It has no reality but on the earth's plane. It is used as an excuse of ours to convince us of our vulnerability to attack and to make death a reality for us.

Truth - The knowledge that GOD IS.

Thoughts - Mind energy is what the universe is made of and thoughts rule creation. Thought is manifested in the third dimensional reality. It is essential that humanity understand this for its spiritual growth. "All thinking produces form at some level." **(ACIM)** Thoughts are things. They manifest in the ethers first then in physical form. They are not neutral.

White Light of Protection - This is a form of spiritual energy that we can invoke for our protection at any time. You can visualize this White Light and bring it into your third dimensional world for healing, peace and empowerment. You can surround your children, home, car, or personal effects with it at all times. I teach my Reiki students, young and old alike, to invoke it when in any adverse situation. Energy of a lesser vibration cannot penetrate this shield of White Light. You become invisible to any harm.

Recommended Reading

A Course in Miracles. Tiburon, CA: Foundation for Inner Peace, 1975.

Baldwin, Judith A. and William. *From My Heart to Yours: A Transformational Guide to Unlocking the Power of Love*. Terra Alta, W.V.: Headline Books, Inc. 1997.

Baldwin, Judith. *The Inner Knower.* Beth Publications, 1996 and *Techniques Manual*, 2nd Ed. Terra Alta, W.V.: Headline Books, Inc 1992.

Benner, Joseph. *The Impersonal Life.* P. O. Box 550, Marina Del Ray, CA: DeVorss & Co., 1941.

Cady, Emilie. *How I Used Truth.* Lee Summit, MO: Unity School of Christianity Publishers, 1950.

Cameron, Fred and Pam. *Bridge Into Light.* Livermore, CA: Oughten House Publications, 1991, 1994.

Doolin, Chris and Daya Devi-. *Hidden Manna.* Ayer, MA: Eternal Publications, 1981.

Doolin, Daya Devi-Rev. *Dabney's Handbook on A Course in Miracles*. Enterprise, FL: Padaran Publications, 1989.

Doolin, Daya Devi-Rev. *All I Need To know...Is Inside*. Enterprise, FL: Padaran Publications, 1989.

Gerber, Richard, M.D. *Vibrational Medicine.* Santa Fe, NM: Bear & Company Publishing, 1988.

Jampolsky, Gerald G., M.D. *Love is Letting Go of Fear.* New York, NY: Bantam Books, 1979.

Laut, Phil. *Money Is My Friend.* San Rafael, Ca: Trinity Publications, 1978.

Long, Max Freedom. *The Secret Science Behind Miracles: Unveiling the Huna Tradition of the Ancient Polynesians.* Marina del Ray, CA: DeVorss & Company, 1948, 1976.

Luk, A.D. *Law of Life, Vol. I & II.* Pueblo, CO: A.D. Luk Publications, 1960.

Levine, Barbara Hoberman. *Your Body Believes Every Word You Say.* Santa Rosa, CA: Aslan Publishing, 1991.

Marciniak, Barbara. *Bringers of the Dawn.* Santa Fe, NM: Bear & Company Publishing, 1992.

Mandino, Og. *The Greatest Secret In The World.* New York, NY: Bantam Books, Inc., 1972.

Nelson, Ruby. *The Door of Everything.* Marina Del Ray, CA: DeVorss & Company, 1963.

Ponder, Catherine. *Pray and Grow Rich.* Marina Del Ray, CA: DeVorss & Company, 1968.

Price, John Randolph. *Super Beings.* Austin, TX: Quartus Foundation, 1981.

Ray, Sondra. *The Only Diet There Is.* Berkeley, CA: Celestial Arts, 1981.

The Reiki Journal. American International Reiki. Santa Monica, CA.

Robbins, Anthony. *Unlimited Power.* New York, NY: Simon and Schuster, 1986.

Walsch, Neal Donald. *Conversations With God.* New York, NY: *G.P. Putnum's Sons,* 1996.

Index

A

B

C

G

H

I

J

K

L

M

P

Q

R

S

T

U

V

W

About the Author

Daya Devi-Doolin has literally slept in abandoned, rat infested condemned buildings, under apartment tenant's cars, in wooded parks, city park benches, under boardwalk planks with her husband Chris. She is a living example of what she writes because she has been without food, housing, clothes and she was separated from her first son for awhile.

Daya Devi-Doolin is a warm, humorous, wonderful person, full of Light, love and nurturing. She is compassionate with everyone.

She is an Ordained Priest of the Melchizedek Order that is involved in the renewing of our planet. She is the Co-Founder and Director of The Doolin Healing Sanctuary located in Enterprise, FL and is President and Co-owner of Padaran Publications. She is a Certified Usui Reiki Master Teacher, a Rebirther, having been trained by the Sondra Ray method and a graduate of Sondra Ray's LRT (Loving Relationship Training) program.

Rev. Daya Devi-Doolin is an author, lecturer, keynote speaker and co-facilitator with her husband Chris, of The Course (A Course in Miracles), Dream Study groups and a singer songwriter-musician. As a duo, they give concerts under the name of Level Seven. She and Chris offer spiritual counseling, lead workshops, study groups and seminars on various metaphysical topics to help prosper and encourage others to witness their full potential. Daya has two sons, Tyler and Joseph. She and her family reside in Enterprise, Florida.

ATTENTION HEALING CENTERS, SCHOOLS OF SPIRITUAL GROWTH, AND ORGANIZATIONS: Quantity discounts are available on bulk purchases of this book for educational purposes or fund raising. For information, please contact Padaran Publications, Box 4267, Enterprise, FL 32725-0267 or call (407) 668-9884. For individuals, please fill out the coupon below and return it payable to Padaran Publications. We thank you for your support and bless you in your total growth.

Super Vita-Minds

Please send me { } copies Super Vita-Minds @ $21.95 each.
Plus applicable sales tax and $3.00 Postage & Handling.
Allow 6-8 weeks for delivery.
Name:__________
Address__________
City:__________
State:__________
Zip Code:__________
Telephone:__________
Visa/MC #:__________Expir. Date:__________
Signature:__________

Price may change without notice.
Please send checks/money orders Padaran Publications
Visa/MC orders to: The Doolin Healing Sanctuary
P. O. Box 4267
Enterprise, FL 32725-0267
(407) 668-9884

PADARAN PUBLICATIONS
ORDER FORM FOR OTHER BOOKS WRITTEN BY REV. DAYA DEVI-DOOLIN

ITEM #	QTY.	TITLE
DH20		All I Need To Know....Is Inside $8.95
DH21		Dabney's Handbook on ***ACIM***, (illus.) $12.95
DH22		Dormck (children's book) $4.95
DH23		Dormck and the Temple of the Healing Light, (children's book) $9.95
DH24		Returning to the Source (book of poems) $3.50
DH25		Sikado's Star of Aragon, (Another Dormck adventure children's book) $9.95
DH26		Dabney, Dormck & Wiggles' Slakaduman Adventure, (children's book) $9.95
		Sub-total
		Sales tax
		Shipping & Handling $3.00
		Total Cost

Please send checks/money orders Padaran Publications
Visa/MC orders to: The Doolin Healing Sanctuary
P. O. Box 4267
Enterprise, FL 32725-0267
(407) 668-9884

Level Seven

"...Theirs is a winning performance!"
Thomas Duffy, Orlando Sentinel

Cassette "*Swept Away*"'

Order Form for Cassettes and CD's

Please send me ___Tape(s) @ $10.00 each Ship. & Hdlg. $1 ea.
Name
Address Phone
City/State/Zip
Check/M.O.
Signature

Send to:
Padaran Publications
P. O. Box 4267
Enterprise, FL 32725-0267 (407) 668-9884
Email: cdoolin@bitstorm.net